Black Sea
Caspian Sea
Samsun
Istanbul
Trabzon
Erzurum
Mt Ararat
Ankara
TURKEY
Tabriz
Tehran
SYRIA
IRAQ
IRAN
The Gulf of Oman
Red Sea
SAUDI
ARABIA

FOUR WHEELS & FRONTIERS

ROY FOLLOWS CPM FRGS

FOREWORD
Rt Hon Lord Steel of Aikwood KBE PC DL

ISBN 0-9537577-8-1

ULRIC PUBLISHING
P.O.BOX 55 CHURCH STRETTON SHROPSHIRE SY6 6WR ENGLAND
TELEPHONE: 44(0)1694 781354 FACSIMILE: 44(0)1694 781372

e-mail: books@ulricpublishing.com
www.ulricpublishing.com

CONTENTS

The names of countries referred to in this publication, relate to the year the journey was made.

THE RT HON LORD STEEL OF AIKWOOD KBE PC DL

HOUSE OF LORDS

LONDON SW1A 0PW

Having successfully completed (with bronze medallion) the 1998 "drive of a lifetime" from London to Cape Town in a 1965 Austin Gipsy, I am full of wondrous admiration at the feat of Roy Follows and Noel Dudgeon.

Their vehicle seems to have been even more basic than ours, and they did the drive from Singapore to London, not as we did in a rally well organised by the Historic Endurance Rally Organisation but entirely on their own, with limited map information through wild uncharted territories.

This volume is of wider interest than just to old car nuts like me. It is an adventure story of human ingenuity, a unique travelog unlikely ever to be repeated.

David Steel August 2004

ACKNOWLEDGEMENTS

With the exception of Willys USA, who provided details on the model of Jeep, plus a workshop manual and letter of encouragement, the journey from Singapore to England was undertaken without corporate support: in short there are no sponsors or back-up teams to acknowledge.

In sharp contrast, we are indebted to many diverse individuals. Without the generosity of these real people – from diplomats to bullock-cart drivers, this 13,000 -mile venture would have been less colourful, and undoubtedly failed. The small acts of kindness that helped us on our way are infinite:

Without the enthusiasm of Soong, the Chinese scrap merchant, we would have never considered buying the wreck of a Jeep. Angela Khoo, at our Police HQ in Johore, typed endless letters in preparation for the journey. The Burmese Police Inspector in Thaton offered the safety of his police compound and supplied a couple of rifles for the night. A clean, dry bed, provided by a Burmese missionary station, was a rare and welcomed luxury. Without the help of Captain Tun, who agreed to trade a few gallons of petrol, we would have had to walk to India.

Over in the remote corner of northeast India, warm fruit, broken biscuits and a can of petrol, were greatly received from the staff of the North East Frontier Agency. The English employees, and hardy drinkers at the Digboi Oil Company, rallied around to exchange rupees for sterling currency. Having accidentally driven into a tea planter's garden in Assam, we received an impromptu invitation to join the family dinner party and stay the evening.

In Darjeeling, it would be hard to better the generous hospitality of Major Amos and the Gurkhas. Then there's the drunken, Indian cyclist, who gave me a hitch, along with a drum of oil: he is warmly remembered for his sheer determination.

Moving further west, the mechanics in Pakistan who welded the cracked chassis. Over in Iran, we quenched our thirst with endless cups of sweet, black tea from the Iranian police, while garage owner Dimitri, pulled out all the stops to get us up and running yet again.

Turkey will be remembered for the British Ambassador who ensured our passports were returned from the Yugoslav Embassy. In Belgrade, we received exceptional hospitality from our friend Paddy and his colleagues at the British Embassy.

Our independent efforts to acquire Burmese visas failed. Thanks to the expediency of Jack Slater (our boss and Chief of Police for Johore), Fred Warner from the British Embassy, Rangoon, and a senior employee in Malay Police Special Branch, the Burmese eventually conceded.

The spontaneous generosity of my platoon who donated their surplus tinned rations - a crucial food supply for the journey, along with the moral support of our friends in the Malay Police, more than compensated for lack of sponsorship.

Finally, the miscellaneous individuals scraping a living at so many roadside food stalls, who kindly exchanged snacks for fags, enabling us to stave off our hunger. We will always be indebted to these people, plus of course the ones who have been accidentally omitted. A simple 'thank you' seems weak and inadequate, but as there are no other words;

thank you.

DEDICATION

The other half of this overland adventure was my firm and special friend, Noel Dudgeon – a man of the highest calibre, who without being flippant never failed to resolve the most dangerous situations. Even under the most severe conditions Noel never complained; well, perhaps a little when his fags were wet. Today's familiar terms, 'stressed' and 'under pressure' are just not in Noel's vocabulary. No one could wish for a better person at their side in a perilous situation, and I consider myself blessed to have shared the tribulations and pleasures of this journey with him.

Highly intelligent and quick to seize the initiative, should plan 'A' fail, Noel was always ready with plan 'B' and even 'C.' It was in the hostile world of the Malay jungle, where the wretched conditions quickly expose character flaws and sort the wheat from the chaff, that Noel and I came to know each other. On dangerous under-cover operations, when tested to our limits, we worked well together, respected each other's opinion, and never once fell out, and mutual reliability was implicit, regardless of circumstances.

Noel's remarkable sense of humour was always on top form in the most dangerous situations, where his witty one-liners made an incident such as an ambush, appear like an everyday event. Noel's easy-going disposition, combined with a tall, slim stature, belied an inner toughness and bulldog-like tenacity.

Thanks, Noel.

PLIEUT I
FM

CHAPTER 1

BLIGHTY OR BUST

Police HQ Johore Bahru. Left to right: Chief of Police Johore - Jack Slater, Roy Follows, Assistant Chief of Police - Pat Goldsburg, Noel Dudgeon.

CHAPTER 1

BLIGHTY OR BUST

The wheels of the Jeep spun, sinking deeper into the swamp. Noel slammed it into four-wheel-drive. The engine roared, filling the jungle with exhaust fumes. Trapped up to the axles, the Jeep lurched forward and in a vain attempt to escape, its wheels whisked the mud into a bubbling gruel.

'No good, it's another winch job.' Noel cut the engine.

More problems, I thought, as the acrid smell of an over-heated clutch caught my nostrils. It was mid-morning on our second day of driving through the little-known jungles of southern Thailand, and a week since we'd set off from Singapore. The warnings from numerous sceptics who'd said we must be mad and that the journey was impossible had already started to plague us.

Twelve months had passed since Noel and I had shunned the idea of cruising home to England aboard a P & O liner, or flying BOAC. Just for the hell of it, we'd decided to drive the 13,000 miles from Singapore to England. [1]

While serving as Colonial Police officers in the Malay Emergency, we'd been engaged on highly sensitive jungle operations against the Communist guerrillas. The idea of driving back to England was first mooted during one of our joint operations. In our jungle lair, over a meal of rice and dried fish, we talked about our forthcoming leave. Although some twelve months away, Police HQ had already issued the travel details, which included the option of returning home by sea or air.

'I think I'll go by air this time, instead of a slow boat.' Noel picked at his rice.

'What about you, Roy? You've done the sea voyage a number of times during your Merchant Navy days. Flying to England will be a change.'

'What about overland?' I quipped, chewing on a wad of salted fish and running the spoon around my mess tin, chasing the last few grains of rice.

'Overland. Driving. Is it possible?' Noel dug in his rucksack for cigarettes, took a burning brand from the fire and lit up.

'I don't know, never gave it a thought until now, but it sounds more exciting than going by ship or plane.'

Seeing Noel's reaction, I knew he was already hooked on the idea. Suddenly this light-hearted banter had become a serious proposition. That evening, in our jungle hideout, we talked of nothing but the possibility of driving back to England. To minimise expenses, we were hoping to persuade Police HQ to give us cash instead of travel tickets for the passage home.

Early the following morning, we set up an ambush close to a disused track on the jungle's edge. This ambush was significantly different, since our orders were not to 'eliminate,' but to 'capture.' We'd also been informed by Special Branch that members of the Communist organisation used the track several times a week.

Noel and I usually operated independently with our own platoons. However, given the 'risky business' of this particular ambush, we'd been asked to do the job together, along with several Chinese men from Noel's platoon.

'A year from now, Noel, we could be motoring through Thailand,' I whispered, swigging from my water bottle. *'Water?'*

'No thanks, Roy, but I could murder a cigarette.' Noel peered through the undergrowth, knowing his next smoke would have to wait until the ambush was over.

He didn't have to wait long; as I clipped the bottle back onto my belt, I was distracted by a movement in the undergrowth. Focusing on the direction of the sound, my fingers crawled along the butt of my automatic towards the trigger. As the noise in the undergrowth became more apparent, I could just pick out the red star on the cap of a Communist guerrilla moving cautiously towards me. His khaki uniform was darkened with patches of perspiration, and his weapon, at the ready.

When I raised a thumb to Noel he mouthed an 'OK' in return. As the Communist drew closer, I could hear the leather of his equipment creak, and noticed his boots were slung around his neck. Noel and I glanced at each other, then nodding the 'go,' burst out of the foliage and bundled him over before he had chance to use his weapon. While he was lying on his back with the muzzle of Noel's automatic rammed in his guts, we relieved him of his Sten gun, then searched his pockets for identification.

'A good catch, we'll get him to Special Branch as soon as possible.' Noel tapped a cigarette from the packet and flicked his lighter into action.

I was based and operating in north Johore, while Noel was in the south of Malaya, so weeks went by before we managed to meet up again. During this time, our application for cash instead of complimentary tickets home was approved. The payment, however, was conditional on completing the journey and personally collecting our respective cheques from the Crown Offices in London.

Now that the main finances were arranged, we pressed ahead with our planning. When we studied numerous weather graphs and maps, it became clear that it was essential to plan the expedition around the monsoon season to avoid being trapped by the monsoons of Southeast Asia and India.

We aimed for February 1st as our departure day, since it fell in line with preferable weather patterns and allowed us nine months to organise. Given that we were both constantly on jungle operations, and only had a few days' break each month, this wasn't actually very long.

The spin-off from these monthly 'jungle ops' meant that we could build up additional ration packs for the trip. The process was quite easy; when asking for an air supply of food and other essential items in deep jungle, we inflated the number of men in our respective platoons. Surprisingly, no one ever queried why the amount of rations we ordered was disproportionate to the length of the operation or the number of men.

By repeatedly ordering 'extras,' my room back at HQ soon became stacked with enough canned food for most of the journey. We also acquired socks, shirts, plus a bright green parachute, which was made into endless pairs of disposable underpants.

Our choice of vehicle was quickly narrowed down to a British Land Rover, or American Willys Jeep. Both vehicles had the essential four-wheel-drive. Used by the military and police in Malaya, many Land Rovers were armour-plated, however, it would be difficult, if not impossible, to buy Land Rover spares in the remote areas we'd be driving through.

Although not ideal for long haul expeditions, - amongst other things it didn't have doors, the Willys Jeep, the vehicle of choice for the American and British Military, was used extensively in Burma and India during the Second World War, and therefore the likelihood of tracking down spares would be greater.

'Soong and Company, Dealers In Scrap Motor Vehicles & Spare Parts. Johore Bahru.' Noel and I read the weathered notice-board from his much-loved Alvis Coupé and drove into the compound of rusting vehicles where a pack of snarling dogs exploded in front of the car.

O.C. No:9 S.O.V.F.
CONTINGENT S.B. HEADQUARTERS,
J O H O R E.

15 JUNE'57.

Director,
Of Ordnance Services,
G.H.Q.,
c/o G.P.O., SINGAPORE.

<u>Ref: PP/2</u>

Sir,

I have been advised to write to you for help regarding the possible purchase of a secondhand jeep from the Military authorities.

My friend and I early next year intend to attempt the return trip to the United Kingdom overland, via SIAM and BURMA. The only vehicle which of course could be used for this, would be either a Jeep or a Landrover, and the running costs for the 15,000 mile journey make the purchase of a new vehicle a little beyond our means.

We realise of course that quite a sum of money would have to be spent on a vehicle supplied by the Military, before it could be used for the purpose in view, but feel in the end this would be cheaper.

I am writing at this early date, as if such a purchase is possible, we wish to have at least six months to work on the jeep, replacing and repairing parts, before the final move.

Any advice at all you can give us on how one purchases a W.D. Vehicle will be most gratefully received.

Thanking you in anticipation.

I am Sir,

Your obedient servant,

(N.B. DUDGEON).

Letter to the director of Ordnance Services, Singapore, regarding the purchase of a Jeep.

Major W.J. SMITH RAOC
ORD Directorate
GHQ FARELF.

FE 61133 ORD 5.

24th June 57.

Dear Mr DUDGEON.

I am writing in response to your PP/2 dated 15 June 57 and without wishing to paint too difficult a picture on the question of Jeep provision I ~~and~~ would point out the following regulations etc.

(a) War Department Depots are not allowed to sell any surplus vehicle to other than registered second hand dealers and all sales are reported to the police.

(b) Neither the Federation or the Singapore Government will now licence a left hand drive vehicle.

(c) The only vehicles sold as surplus to Army requirements are in Class III or lower condition ie are by no means good runners.

There is of course no problem in buying a jeep from second hand dealers but you may have difficulty in licensing and some expense when putting the thing on the road.

Yours faithfully

Mr. DUDGEON,
OC No.9 SOVF,
CONTINGENT S.B. HEADQUARTERS,
J O H O R E.

Reply from Major W.J.Smith, Ordnance Services.

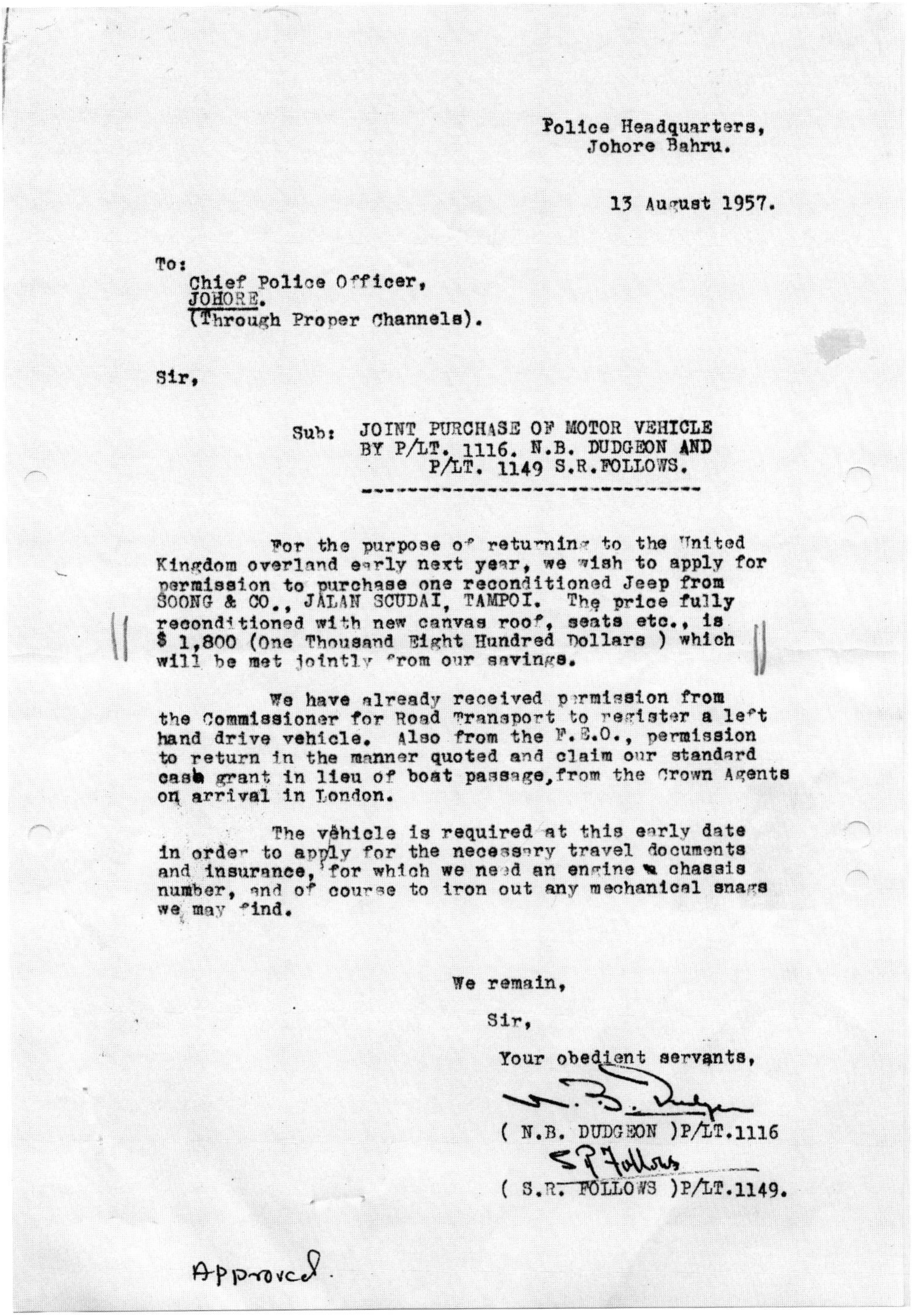

Police Headquarters,
Johore Bahru.

13 August 1957.

To:

Chief Police Officer,
JOHORE.
(Through Proper Channels).

Sir,

Sub: JOINT PURCHASE OF MOTOR VEHICLE BY P/LT. 1116. N.B. DUDGEON AND P/LT. 1149 S.R.FOLLOWS.

For the purpose of returning to the United Kingdom overland early next year, we wish to apply for permission to purchase one reconditioned Jeep from SOONG & CO., JALAN SCUDAI, TAMPOI. The price fully reconditioned with new canvas roof, seats etc., is $ 1,800 (One Thousand Eight Hundred Dollars) which will be met jointly from our savings.

We have already received permission from the Commissioner for Road Transport to register a left hand drive vehicle. Also from the F.E.O., permission to return in the manner quoted and claim our standard cash grant in lieu of boat passage, from the Crown Agents on arrival in London.

The vehicle is required at this early date in order to apply for the necessary travel documents and insurance, for which we need an engine & chassis number, and of course to iron out any mechanical snags we may find.

We remain,

Sir,

Your obedient servants,

N. B. Dudgeon

(N.B. DUDGEON)P/LT.1116

S R Follows

(S.R. FOLLOWS)P/LT.1149.

Approved.

Letter to the Chief Police Officer, Johore, requesting permission to buy a reconditioned Jeep from Soong & Co.

'No. No hurt you. No hurt you.' A short, jovial character, with a mahogany-coloured paunch, disguised beneath the remains of a tattered grey vest dispersed the pack.

'No hurt you, only give you rabies.' Noel countered as they slunk away. We tentatively climbed out of the car, into the scorching heat. Noel, who spoke Cantonese, made the introductions. The 'dog handler' was Mr Soong, who ran the company with his two sons.

'First time I do business with English men. Come, come my house.' Pulling up his loose shorts, he led us through the maze of decaying vehicle parts towards his clapboard home.

A solitary light bulb peppered with insect droppings hovered precariously over a table littered with mah-jong tiles, and ashtrays, while in the far corner a makeshift shrine pulsed out a sickly, joss-stick fragrance. During the course of the next few months, Soong's home became the dealing den where we spent hours haggling over the cost of Jeep repairs and modifications. Conveniently, when the conversation turned to money, his English rapidly improved and he became the 'poor man' with hungry children to feed.

'Sit, sit down.' Soong pulled up a couple of stools, and we started to explain what we were looking for while he leaned back in his rattan chair with his brow knitted together.

Drive to England? I have Bedford lolly, three tonner, good condition. Special price to you.' He fingered a black hair protruding from his chin. Soong evidently drove a hard bargain, but all the same, couldn't grasp what we were taking on.

'We're after a Jeep, not a lorry.' Noel offered him a cigarette.

'Have good army Jeep, but no working.' Soong offered, then, sucking on the butt of his cigarette, coughed and deposited a pearl of phlegm into the enamel spittoon next to his chair.

'Repair Jeep no problem, I have good mechanics.'

Our hearts sank when we first set eyes on the drab-olive Jeep, which had apparently been dumped in the scrapyard for over six months. All the tyres, including the spare, were flat. The canopy hung in tatters, and the horsehair filling was bursting out of the wafer-thin seats. Lifting up the bonnet we expected to see entrails of wire and the remains of a cannibalised engine, but surprisingly it was intact; there was no evidence of leaks from the cooling system, and the oil was clean and at the correct level.

Noel unclipped the axe and spade, which were in near-mint condition.[2] The same went for the jerry can: the filling cap and securing buckle were both seized-up with paint,and may have never been used. The British Army 'HQ' logo stencilled on one of the side panels indicated the Jeep was formerly an army staff vehicle, and therefore well serviced. Our spirits began to rise.

'What do you think?' Soong hovered around, praising the wreck, while Noel climbed into the driving seat.

'Not exactly a Rolls – a bit cramped.' Noel's 6-foot 2-inch frame hunched over the steering wheel. *'But it's sturdy – just what we want, what's your opinion Roy?'*

'If the price is right, we'll take it.'

'You like?' Soong flashed a mouthful of brassy-looking teeth. *'I make special price for my English friends.'*

'Look!' I tore a piece off the canopy. *'This is rotten, and the tyres are perished. It's a load of old junk.'*

'Junk?' Soong looked puzzled. *'This Jeep, no boat.'*

'Yes, don't worry.' Not wanting to confuse the issue, I quickly agreed and pitched the crucial question. *'What price you ask?'*

'Come, we go house, talk business, have drink.' The haggling was about to begin.

'Yam Sing!' Soong raised a glass of Cognac, before downing it in one go.

'Cheers!' We swiftly knocked back a couple of glasses of brandy.

'Special offer, 2,000 dollar.[3] ' Soong belched, wafting garlic-laden breath into my face.

'No way,'

'What you give, then?' The palm of his hand soothed his fat, brown belly.

'I've never met a Chinese Jew before,' I teased. *'It's only worth 1,250 dollars.'*

'Chinese Jew!' Tickled by the remark, he reached for his abacus and proceeded to flick the beads along the rods. *'Can't do. What about 1,850?'* He peered over the rim of his glass in anticipation.

'Still too dear.'

The haggling and heat in the room intensified as we chipped more and more off the price. Some two hours and many brandies later, we beat Soong down to 1,750 Malay dollars. Just one hundred dollars stood between us when stalemate set in. Feigning to leave, we thanked him for his hospitality, and drained our glasses.

'No no, please sit down, don't go. 'We can reach some agreement.' His trembling hands refilled the glasses.

'Yam Sing! Soong tipped back another brandy and sent a board of mah-jong tiles scattering across the table as he banged down his empty glass.

Three more brandies later, with his senses dulled and abacus beads a blur, he accepted our offer of 1,800 dollars. This included 1,550 Malay dollars for the Jeep plus 250 Malay dollars for a complete overhaul and spares. We agreed to pay the money in cash, with an initial 10 per cent up front; Soong couldn't take cheques since he didn't have a bank account.

'When you come back from jungle, Jeep will be stripped down.' He slurred, and we reluctantly paid the deposit, shook hands and departed.

Five days later, my platoon and I were struggling through a waist-deep tidal mangrove swamp on the east coast of Malaya. We were covered in leeches and constantly under attack from mosquitoes. It was also the monsoon season, and raining incessantly. With our jungle shelter offering little protection from hurricane-force downpours, the nights were long, cold, and wet.

After three weeks of amphibian-like living, I went down with severe malaria. Having malaria anywhere is bad enough, but on a muddy islet in a mangrove, without appropriate medication or even the basic home comforts, its absolute misery. I lay unwashed and delirious in my slime-soaked combat gear for about three days and then, with the help of my platoon, trekked through the swamp to a small fishing village. Unaware this would be my last jungle operation, we rested here for another couple of days before staggering back to our HQ in Johore.

I'd contracted malaria a number of times, and was therefore advised to take a break from jungle life, (then transferred to the Police Marine Branch in Johore Bahru once I'd reovered). This new post was a great boost to planning our journey; Noel was also based in Johore, which meant we could both visit Soong to check out the progress on the Jeep. My new job also involved regular trips to Singapore, where I was able to buy a whole range of items for our venture from Thieves' Market.

Soong was propped up against the wreck of a Triumph Mayflower enjoying a smoke when I first drove into the yard. I'd been granted a few days' sick leave, and feeling infinitely better, had taken the opportunity to pay him a visit.

'Hey! What's wrong? You look ill, you need blandy.' He stubbed his cigarette butt into the ground with his crusty bare foot. *'Dogs locked up.'* He sensed my apprehension as I stepped from the car.

'No thanks, Soong. Getting over malaria, alcohol not recommended while on medication.'

'Malaria! Cooked dog flesh good, have you tried?'

'Could have, I don't know. When sick in the jungle, I'm past caring what my Chinese orderly gives me for a cure.'

'Could be monkey.' He laughed,slapping the bonnet of my car. 'A*h! Standard Vanguard, go quick. You see Mayflower?'* He pointed towards the black Triumph. *'Chinese won't buy them, shape too much like a hearse, a Malay wrecked this one. Where's your friend ? He speak my language.'*

'Still in the jungle?' For security reasons I glossed over the details. Noel and his platoon were actually carrying out a sophisticated operation which, if successful, would result in the death of many senior Communist guerrillas in Johore.

'Jungle no good, Communist no good.' Soong spat on the floor in contempt. *'If they win, they take my business, me finish.'* He drew the edge of his hand in a cutting gesture across this throat.

Like the majority of Chinese in Malaya, Soong was afraid of a Communist takeover. With their hard-work ethic and business skills, the Chinese had become the backbone of the Malay economy. Most businesses, including rubber estates and tin mines were controlled by the Chinese.

After I'd assured him the Communists were on the edge of defeat, he led me over to the workshop, where the Jeep was stripped down to its last nut and bolt. The transmission, radiator, wheels, brakes, and pistons lay in an orderly fashion on the ground.

'This is Chang. A good worker, when not on the opium.' An emaciated body curled over the cylinder head.

'OK, Chang?' I enquired, uneasy that a drug addict was overhauling the Jeep. He nodded and scurried beneath the engine bay.

Back at Soong's home, jars of burning joss sticks were still emitting their heady fragrance, and since our previous visit, bowls of fruit had been placed on the shrine as gifts to the spirits.

Soong plucked a cigarette from a battered packet and a young, willowy Chinese woman, dressed in a figure-hugging cheongsam appeared with a tray of coffee balanced between perfectly manicured hands. When Soong thanked her, she made a calculated move towards the door, 'accidentally' exposed her thigh, then disappeared.

'Your daughter?' I sipped the sweet, black coffee.

'Daughter! Mr Roy, you think daughter? No daughter. She my concubine.' His eyes disappeared as he attempted a knowing wink. '*She 17-year-old cherry girl, I get special price – bargain. Same you get Jeep.*' Soong had an answer for everything.

We tried to clinch a number of sponsorship deals but they were all unsuccessful. Shell Oil declined sponsorship on the grounds that many of the places along our route werere not covered by their outlets, and as such we'd be obliged to fill up with a rival company's fuel. All the other international petroleum companies believed the journey would be impossible to complete. At Firestone Tyres in Singapore, the European executive, who had little knowledge of the Malay Emergency, showed his irreverence by offering a cheap, promotional tyre gauge.

One afternoon, Noel and I headed for the offices of the Singapore Automobile Association with the aim of buying good maps and seeking advice on various road conditions. If the tide was out, on leaving Johore Bahru and crossing the bridge over the river, there was always an unbearable stench. The water, which was lumpy with sewage, slithered onto the shore a few yards down from the bridge, waiting to be dispersed by the tide. Just sniffing-distance away were a couple of restaurants noted by the locals for their excellent fresh seafood. Although the fish was caught near the sewage discharge, I also frequented these restaurants but surprisingly never contracted food poisoning.

Within minutes of passing through Johore's town centre we crossed the causeway linking Malaya to Singapore, then went on to the Bukit Tima Road and the urban outskirts of Singapore. Roadside hawkers, with dextrous, bony fingers surrounded the car at every opportunity offering sweetmeats wrapped in banana leaves, and neon-coloured fruit drinks balanced on palettes of crushed ice. Having negotiated our way through a labyrinth of narrow streets, simmering with a kaleidoscope of characters all going in different directions, and invariably on the wrong side of the road, we arrived at the AA office.

'Trip to England? We're here to help. Do you wish to disembark at Madras or Bombay?' The Chinese clerk peered over his spectacles. *'The British Indian Shipping Line operate a good service between Singapore and India but there are others.'*

Noel shrugged his shoulders. *'Sorry – you've misunderstood.* We intend to drive to England.*'*

'But,' he removed his spectacles, *'first of all you have to go by ship to India, and I strongly recommend the British India Line. I suggest you book early.'*

The clerk was genuinely concerned about our well-being and, listened intently, occasionally shaking his head in disbelief, when we explained our plan.

'What about the jungles of southern Thailand? You couldn't survive if you broke down there. It would be impossible to rescue you – have you thought about that? Then there's Burma. The journey's impossible.'

A hint of a smile crossed Noel's face. I knew what was going through his mind. We were both conditioned to jungle hostilities; we'd often been lost with our platoons in uncharted territory for days and always found our way out, avoiding casualties and Communist attack. For security reasons, particularly for Noel, who was often engaged on special operations with his platoon of ex-Chinese Communist guerrillas, it was prudent not to mention our history.

'That contingency is covered – emergency kit – our rucksacks, already packed with five days' food, and survival items,' Noel affirmed. *'If the Jeep becomes trapped in a swamp, submerged in a river, or whatever, we grab our rucksacks and start trekking.'* He spoke in a matter-of-fact way, as if it were a regular occurrence.

'Um, you seem determined, and well organised.' The clerk pushed the shipping file to one side.

'We are, but we need to buy decent maps. For starters, we could do with road maps of Thailand and Burma.' I opened my wallet.

'Buy two of each in case we lose any Roy. The spares can go with our survival kit.' Noel was on the ball as usual, always prepared for the unexpected, but in this instance his foresight was of little use.

'Sorry, the AA can't help you. There are no decent roads in southern Thailand, therefore no road maps for this area, and the Burmese won't grant you an entry visa under any conditions. You should seriously consider booking a sea passage to India.'

As a last resort, we were put in contact with an army officer in the cartographic department at Military HQ Singapore, but he was posted back to England before he could lay his hands on any relevant maps. He did however give us some excellent, detailed maps of Nepal and the Tibetan border but these places weren't on our itinerary.

Owing to the limited availability of Maps for Burma and Thailand, we had to depend on a wall map of Southeast Asia. With a scale 63 miles to 1 inch it was almost impossible to navigate along the ill-defined Burmese–Chinese frontier. Similarly, for Iran we only had a pictorial wall map. This was fine for the classroom, but of limited use when trying to navigate across desert wastelands.

After much form-filling, the Jeep was granted 'civilian status' and in turn issued with the number plate JA 6178. The repairs were also in hand, and we were well on target, then as the AA clerk had anticipated, the Burmese Consulate in Singapore 'put in the boot' and refused to issue visas. The decision was based on a stringent policy of not allowing foreigners to travel through Burma.

The entire journey now hinged around this vital endorsement in our passports. It had already taken six months to receive a 'Secret' permit from the Ministry of External Affiars New Delhi, allowing us to enter northern India from Burma. [See page 105]

Word of our trip quickly spread through Police HQ, where a number of senior officers who'd served in Burma and India during the Second World War were of immense help.

When Jack Slater, our boss, and Chief of Police for Johore State heard about our 'Burmese plight' he cut through a pile of red tape and immediately

OUR REF: PP/6

N.B. Dudgeon Esq.,
O.C. No: 9 S.O.V.F.,
Contingent Special Branch Hqrs.,
Johore Bahru,
Malaya.

19th August 1957.

Willys Overland
Export Corporation,
New York, N.Y.,
U.S.A.

Sirs,

In late January next year another Police Officer and myself intend to return overland to the United Kingdom from Malaya, via Thailand, Burma, India, Pakistan, Iran, Turkey, Greece, Yugoslavia, and so across Western Europe.

This journey has been done twice from West to East, by the Oxford and Cambridge Far Eastern Expedition, and by Group Captain Townsend respectively, both parties using new Landrovers. We ourselves, have decided to use a Willys Jeep purchased from the British Army Authorities, for what we believe will be the first East to West trip.

The Jeep, Engine No: PV. 32758, Chassis No: P. 55/V/102 is at present undergoing a thorough overhaul entailing a complete stripdown and re-assemble to replace worn parts.

As a matter of interest we would like to know any information you may have on the history of this vehicle, date of manufacture, where it was first sent to etc. Also we would be most grateful for advice on what you consider would be essential spare parts to take with us on such a trip, and if possible a list of agencies across Asia and Europe where spares could be purchased in the event of a breakdown.

To date, we have not managed to get hold of a maintenance book, or any maintenance instructions at all. These, together with any advice on location of possible faults, would be of immense value if you could possibly supply them to us.

I hope my letter consisting throughout with requests for advice and help, does not impose too much on your time.

Thanking you in anticipation,

I am,

Yours sincerely,

(N.B. DUDGEON)

Letter to Willys-Overland, requesting information on the Jeep purchased from Soong & Co.

WILLYS-OVERLAND EXPORT CORPORATION

CABLE ADDRESS WILLYSEXPORT
ALL STANDARD CODES

TOLEDO 1, OHIO, U.S.A.

AIR MAIL

August 29, 1957

Mr. N. B. Dudgeon
O.C. No. 9 S.O.V.F.
Contingent Special Branch Hqrs.
Johore Bahru
Malaya

Dear Mr. Dudgeon

Your letter of August 19 is acknowledged in regard to your anticipated trip from Malaya to Great Britian.

In noting the engine and serial number of your Jeep we are inclined to believe that it is a model CJ-3B which was assembled by our Indian assembly plant Mahindra & Mahindra Limited, Gateway Building, Apollo Bunder, Bombay, India. We suggest you write to them giving them the engine and serial number for the history of the vehicle.

We are attaching hereto a recommended list of spare parts for your trip and a list of distributors under whom dealers operate along your route.

Under separate cover we are forwarding to you the Jeep maintenance manual and operator's manual.

We trust the manuals will be received in due time and that your trip will prove successful.

Very truly yours,

W. V. Kershow

W. V. Kershow
Service Manager

WVK/mmc

Enclosure

AUTHORIZED SERVICE J GENUINE PARTS

Reply from Willys-Overland.

contacted his opposite number in Burma. In turn the Burmese Consulate in Singapore were ordered by the Ministry in Rangoon to issue the visas. The Burmese Consulate were defiant to the end: some eight weeks later, when the visas were stamped in our passports, we were advised they'd only become valid following a further endorsement by the Burmese Embassy in Bangkok.

Once we'd been given the green light for Burma we arranged finances; £200 each as a basic allowance in traveller's cheques.[4] These had to be exchanged at a bank, and a record of the transaction made in our passports. If an enthusiastic frontier official spotted a discrepancy between the number of cheques and the figures written in the passport, we knew the penalties would be severe in some countries.

All the major insurance companies declined our request for cover. However, Caledonian Insurance offered to shoulder our risk and tailored a £20.00 package for six months. Although we were unsure *how* to claim for accidentally knocking down a monk in Mandalay, we did at least have the policy, and it joined our ever-increasing document file

With a full tank of petrol, plus the jerry-can reserve, the fuel range of the Jeep was still insufficient to see us through the long, unknown distances between fuel availability. We also needed to carry water for both the Jeep radiator and drinking. To increase the fuel capacity Soong cannibalised two 15-gallon fuel tanks from a couple of ex-army trucks, and fixed them into the back of the Jeep.

To enable fuel to be transferred without stopping, a tap was fixed onto the fuel line, allowing petrol to be fed from the reserve tanks, through a system of piping and into the main tank. To increase the water capacity, the spare wheel was moved from the back and re-mounted on the right-hand side. A couple of holding brackets were then welded in its place, to which two jerry cans, were secured, one of which had a tap to draw water for a quick brew.

When topped up, we could carry over 42 gallons of petrol, and nine gallons of water, which meant approximately 510 lbs of liquid sloshing about. There was also the camping equipment, spares, plus a modest first-aid kit. To ensure this excessive weight could be carried across some of the roughest terrain in the world, the original leaf springs were replaced with stronger ones.

Soong had gallons of cream paint with little arrows embossed on the tins and the lettering, 'HM Govt, RN' stencilled in black. Although we never found out exactly how he'd acquired it, to avoid ambush by insurgent guerrillas, or so-called 'freedom fighters', we decided to paint the Jeep in

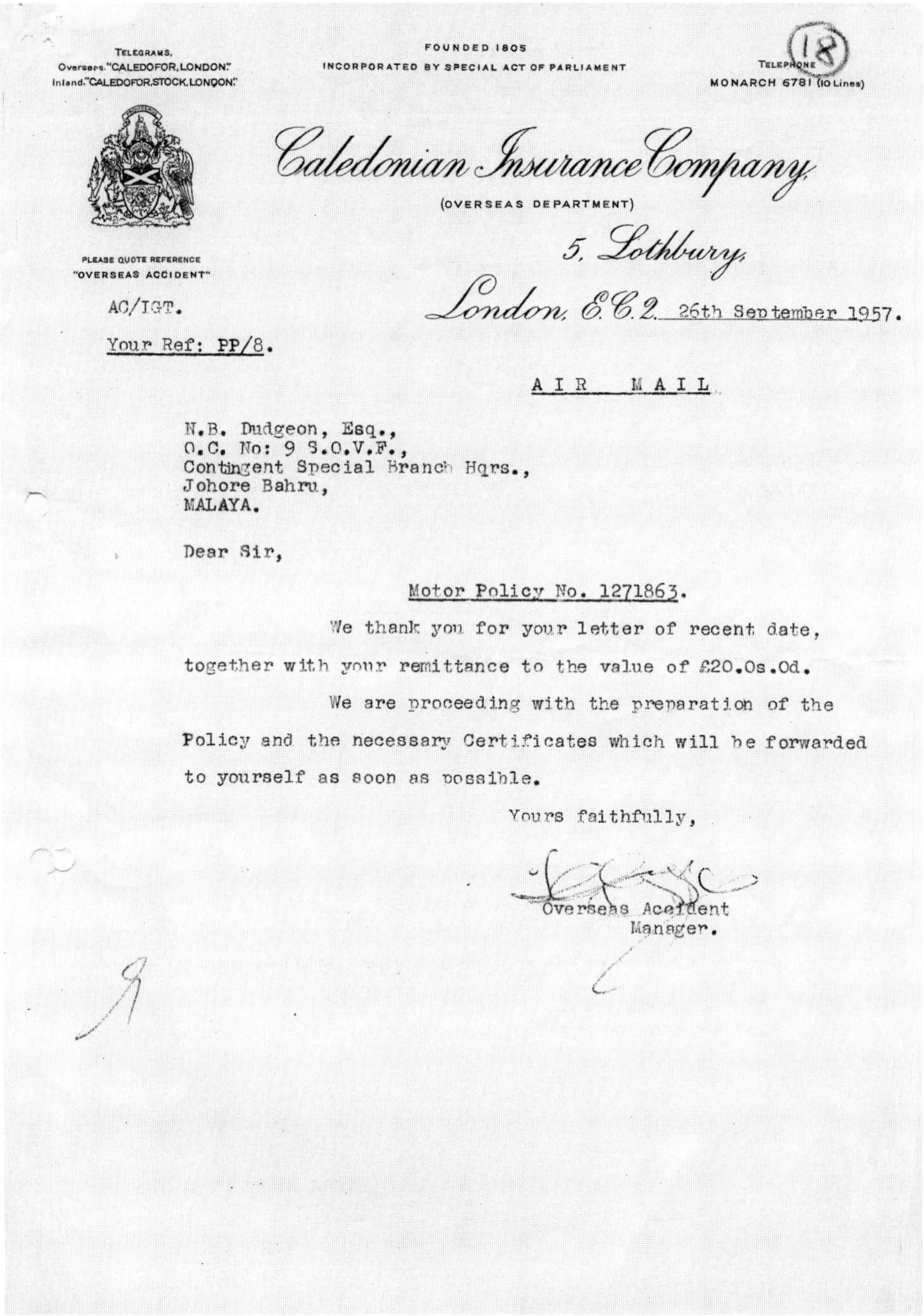
TELEGRAMS.
Overseas."CALEDOFOR, LONDON."
Inland."CALEDOFOR, STOCK, LONDON."

FOUNDED 1805
INCORPORATED BY SPECIAL ACT OF PARLIAMENT

TELEPHONE
MONARCH 6781 (10 Lines)

(18)

Caledonian Insurance Company,
(OVERSEAS DEPARTMENT)

PLEASE QUOTE REFERENCE
"OVERSEAS ACCIDENT"

5, Lothbury,
London, E.C.2. 26th September 1957.

AC/IGT.

Your Ref: PP/8.

A I R   M A I L

N.B. Dudgeon, Esq.,
O.C. No: 9 S.O.V.F.,
Contingent Special Branch Hqrs.,
Johore Bahru,
MALAYA.

Dear Sir,

Motor Policy No. 1271863.

We thank you for your letter of recent date, together with your remittance to the value of £20.0s.0d.

We are proceeding with the preparation of the Policy and the necessary Certificates which will be forwarded to yourself as soon as possible.

Yours faithfully,

Overseas Accident
Manager.

'All the major insurance companies declined our request for cover.'

this impartial cream. With the new black canopy and three jerry cans contrasting sharply with the cream bodywork, it could have easily passed as an ice-cream van.

Arab Street Singapore is the home of the Thieves' Market, where anything can be purchased, on the spot or to order; no questions asked, of course. Bulldozers have disappeared from military establishments, stolen to order, for Arab Street clients in the construction business. In tropical Singapore, it was even possible to buy winter clothing in 'The Street.'

Although we declined the offer of a mint-condition Johnson outboard motor, we ordered most of our supplies from an Arab Street dealer, and collected them the following week for a staggeringly low 'cash no questions' price.[5]

Back at Soong's, after a few minor adjustments, the Jeep passed a two-hour test drive with flying colours. 13,000 miles of adventure lay ahead; all the paperwork was in order, and the equipment meticulously checked. We were ready.

The week before setting off was a constant round of farewell parties, so on the eve of our departure day we planned to have an early, 'no-drinks' night, but when a group of friends from another platoon drove 60 miles from their HQ to drag us out for a final send-off, our good intentions went out of the window. The following morning I awoke with a roaring hangover and realised all the equipment, spare parts and provisions were still scattered around my room.

Despite the suffering from the effects of the previous night, everyone helped to load the Jeep. The hand winch was secured to the front bumper along with ropes, and a can of oil rammed into the footwell on the passenger side. Other things were simply tied on. Once everything was aboard, even without the burden of extra fuel, the Jeep was dangerously down on its suspension.

We knew from our trial runs that the driving position was cramped and uncomfortable, so to give the driver a chance to stretch his legs, we agreed to take turns, spending two hours driving followed by two hours in the passenger seat, navigating. We only expected to stray from this rhythm if one of us became too ill to drive.

The scale and reality of the journey suddenly hit home. In Amy's Bar, our local watering-hole, Amy cracked open a bottle of warm champagne which we drank out of pint mugs – it was that sort of place, then after photographs and innumerable handshakes, we climbed aboard, with Noel taking the wheel.

Above: Noel Dudgeon & Roy Follows with the aptly nicknamed ‘PLIEUT I’ Jeep, recently collected from Soong & Co.

Below: Loading up. The Police Officer’s Mess, Johore Bahru.

After so many setbacks and limited help, our 'off-the-cuff' idea, conceived in a jungle hideout was about to unfold. Noel started the engine, and amid calls of 'Good Luck!' from our friends, we apprehensively pulled away. It was February 1st 1958. A distinct rattle followed the Jeep to the centre of Johore Bahru, where having been gestured to stop by a rickshaw driver, we found several empty oil drums, along with a placard which read 'BLIGHTY OR BUST' suspended to the back of the Jeep.

From Johore, we first headed due south to the infamous Raffles Hotel in Singapore, then doubled back and idled our way north through the Malay peninsula, passing through Kulai Camp, where I said a final goodbye to my jungle mentor and right-hand man, Sergeant Shaffie.

For the first few nights we slept in government rest houses or Police Units where we had friends. In Ipoh, the capital of the rich tin-producing state of Perak, our friends in the 2nd Police Field Force were carrying out cross-border operations deep into the southern Thai jungle, and were

Amy's Bar, our local watering hole, Johore Bahru.
Amy & friend check out the Jeep.

Above: Friends in the 2nd Police Field Force, Perak, Malaya.
Below: Police Lieutenant's Mess, Johore Bahru.
Left to Right: Roy Follows, the cook's wife and Noel Dudgeon.

able to provide up-to-date information regarding Communist activity. Due to its inaccessibility and proximity to Malaya, this area was considered a 'safe haven' for Communists attacking north Malaya: we headed for the southern Thai Jungle in the knowledge there were a number of established Communist guerrilla camps.

During the five days it took to cover the 575 miles to Sadao, the Malay-Thai frontier, the Jeep performed well, and since it didn't have doors, we quickly became adept at anticipating when to 'hang on.'

The Malay-Thai frontier was manned by a couple of police and immigration officials. It was typically colonial in that everything that couldn't move was white-washed, including the stones bordering the tiny garden. We pulled up, next to the horizontal barrier pole.

'Tuan!' It was Razak, a tough character who'd served in my platoon for three years, before malaria took its toll. *'I read all about your journey in the press.'* He was immaculate in highly polished black boots, snow-white gaiters and belt.

'All in order, gentlemen.' The immigration official returned our documents. *'Hope you make it.'* We shook hands.

Razak lifted the barrier. *'Selamat jalan Tuan.'*[6]

'Thanks, Razak.' As we passed through the border into Thailand the asphalt road switched to loose dirt.

A dozen Thai men, all smoking, and in different shades of khaki uniform, slouched outside the dilapidated wooden frontier building. Some had pearl-handled revolvers planted in their belts, others cradled automatics. We handed our papers to a short man, chewing gum. He didn't say much,and like most of his colleagues wore reflector sunglasses. I turned to Noel.

'Tough, mean and moody. He's seen too many films.'

'Haven't they all, Roy.' Noel checked his watch. *'This shouldn't take more than 15 minutes.'* We'd been forewarned about the Thai police, and knew the customary two-hour delay was a bribe tactic.

'Currency! You have plenty US dollar, Yes?' One of the officers snapped, rolling a wad of chewing gum around his mouth. Bribe time had arrived.

'No American dollars.' We lied, hoping he wouldn't do a full search of the Jeep. *'Traveller's cheques, and some ticals, that's all.'*

Sadao.
The Malay-Thai frontier.

Disinterested in our Thai currency, which was no good as a bribe, he ensured our traveller's cheques tallied with the balance in our passports, then conceding to the fact we weren't going to grease palms, feigned to sort through the paperwork.

'What your faith? It's not stated in your passports.' He cut, tapping his gold-veneered teeth with a Parker 51. *'I need to know, to complete these forms.'*

'Church of Turkey.' We snapped, suppressing laughter as he recorded our fictitious religion.

Endnotes

[1] P & O = Peninsular & Orient. BOAC= British Overseas Air Corporation.

[2] The axe and spade and spare jerry can are characteristic trademarks of the Jeep.

[3] 2,000 Malayan dollars was our top price. At the time £1.00 sterling was equal to 8 Malay dollars.

[4] £200.00 was the optimum allowance back in 1958. Traveller's cheques could only be exchanged at banks, which on our route were few and far between.

[5] 2 Duffle coats, 4 British Army tank overalls, 2 pairs of goggles, 1 petrol cooking stove, 1 winch, 1 'lean-to' tent to fasten on the side of the Jeep (custom-made to our rough sketch).

[6] *'Safe journey Sir.'* [Malay translation]

LUCKY MOON

A winch job - Thailand.

CHAPTER 2

LUCKY MOON

Songkhla, a fishing village on the east of the Kra isthmus, came into view after a bumpy two-hour drive. The roads were so inadequate that transport to and from Songkhla had to be by either boat or train; the railway ran from the town centre, north along the coast to Bangkok some 500 miles away.

Having not eaten since the Thai frontier, we stopped at the first opportunity, a bar next to the quay where the 'fish of the day' lay bleaching in the sun adjacent to a small fleet of innocent-looking fishing boats and motorised sampans. On entering the bar through a bat-wing door, we distracted a group of Asians, (possibly smugglers importing cargo from Hong Kong, Macau and the Philippines), sitting at a table piled with dollar notes and empty spirit bottles: Gambling and liquor, a sure recipe for trouble.

'Would you sweet American boys care to order?' A warm hand clamped my shoulder.

'I'm Anthony De Silva, the proprietor. Just call me Tony.' Three identity bracelets chattered on his wrist as his delicate fingers squeezed my upper arm. *'You're a nice, strong boy, what's your name?'*

'Frederick, and Albert.' I inclined my head towards Noel. *'We're English.'*

'Fred and Bert to our friends.' Noel replied, retreating from the silky handshake. De Silva was in his late fifties, of Portuguese descent, with currant-like eyes set in a fleshy, unshaven face.

'Pretty names, I've never met a Fred or a Bert.' Taking a notepad from the pocket of his floral shirt, he jotted down our order, whispered, *'This is on the house, boys.'* then minced away.

Placing the drinks tray on the table with a theatrical flourish, on his return, De Silva made a beeline for Noel. *'Stay the night. We can have fun!'*

Noel recoiled as De Silva's scorpion-like hand sauntered towards his thigh, then the gambling group, fuelled by an excess of liquor, started to thump the table. Trouble was imminent.

Before De Silva had a chance to intervene, a knife was pulled, followed by screams and the sound of shattering glass, as a table sailed through the air towards the window and collided with the ceiling lights. Two bloodstained Orientals grappled with each other in the centre of the room while a couple of kittenish Thai girls scoured the floor and stuffed stray dollar notes into their bras. It was time to exit. Shouting our thanks across to De Silva, who was now more consumed with the fight than our welfare, we headed for the outskirts of Songkhla to find a room for the night.

'I have nice room – clean, you share with monk mens, mosquito net extra. No girlies allowed – make trouble.'

We were speaking to the proprietor of a flophouse who was sitting behind a large teak counter, picking his feet. *'You pay American dollar, eh?'* He looked up from the gnarled foot he was working on.

There was a strong odour about this place, a mixture of spicy cooking and effluent from the open sewer trickling past the door. A decorative altar stretched the length of the main wall, overlooked by a gilt buddha wearing a loincloth and Mona Lisa-like smile.

'Monk mens, who they?' I stressed.

'You gentlemen not know Monk mens?' The proprietor bristled, easing himself out of the chair. *'See buddha – Monk mens.'* Placing his palms together, he faced the altar.

'Ah! Monks?' I sighed, rolling my eyes to the ceiling.

'Yeh! Yeh! Monks.' He forced a smile.

We'd passed a group of monks with saffron-coloured robes and shaven heads, close to this flop-house, shaking their begging bowls and little hand bells.

'*Have you garage we put Jeep?'* We queried as he turned up the speed of the fan and papers fluttered from the counter. *'A place for our Jeep, so it's safe.'*

'Car room.' He rebuked. *'Go to the Lucky Moon coffee shop and see my friend, its not far.'*

Although confused by the sketch map he'd scrawled on a piece of paper, to avoid further rebuke we didn't press for any more directions, and twenty minutes later were outside the Lucky Moon. Like many shops in the

East, it was open-fronted with a pile of hardwood shutters stacked against the wall. At the end of the day, the shutters were slotted into position across the front of the shop, making the building secure. Inside, the walls were painted with yellow, humanoid moons, set against a sky-blue background. The owner, disguised in a cloud of steam, was busily dispensing coffee from a steel urn.

'Do you have car room?' We enquired, sipping gritty, warm coffee.

'No problem. Shop close first.' He assured, creating extra clouds as he tampered with the urn. *'When all the people go, I close shop, you drive Jeep inside.'*

'We drive Jeep into shop. In here?' We queried through suppressed laughter, pointing at the tables.

Several hours later, when the last customer had left, we helped the owner to move the tables and chairs to one side, then drove the Jeep over an open monsoon drain into the shop.

The windowless room I slept in that evening had such a low-angled roof that it was impossible to stand upright. Noel's room, which also had a short bunk covered with a fly-infested mosquito net and stained bedding, faired little better. The toilet was also dubious, with its wooden box full of used toilet paper. An insect-ridden jungle floor is always a more preferable place to sleep than a mattress endorsed with the trademarks of use: I spread my towel across the floorboards, curled up and went to sleep.

The next morning, after the proprietor had filled our flasks, we drove out of the shop, and headed straight to the Highways Department where a bleary-eyed man, who'd clearly overslept, reluctantly answered the door. Two naked toddlers peeked from behind his sarong.

'Sorry to disturb you, but I understand you have the necessary documents so we may continue our journey.'

'Moment, moment.' He gestured for us to wait in his office while he changed into his uniform - a peaked cap, silver-buttoned tunic sporting a lanyard and badges of rank.

'Road permits is it, holidaying, driving around the country?' Sprinkling fish-food into an aquarium of lively fish, he cut an amusing figure since he was barefoot, and the sarong was still wrapped around his legs.

'Yes,we hope to see as much of your beautiful land as possible,' we

fawned. There was an unexpected splash, a frenzy in the tank, as the water seemingly boiled.

'The male fighting fish are always belligerent at feeding time.' He returned to his desk, dusting the last of the food from his hands. *'To take in most of our country I suggest you leave the train at Chumphon, instead of going straight on to Bangkok.'*

'Papers, if you please.' Echoes of the Singapore AA shot through my mind as he opened a duplicating book.

'Yes, we'll take the train to Chumphon.' We lied, having no intention of deviating from our plans.

'You'll find the 'flatcars' for carrying vehicles will be at the rear of the train. There's plenty of time, your train doesn't leave for another two hours, and incidentally it's 03.35 in England.' He stamped the duplicating book, then gave instructions for the travel permit to be countersigned by his opposite number on arrival in Chumphon.

Despite the impressive black stamp and recorded details of the 'proposed' rail journey from Songkhla to Chumphon, this permit was just another insignificant piece of red tape, but we played along: if we'd disclosed our true plans we wouldn't have been given a travel permit. Before leaving we made tentative enquiries about the next stage of our journey, the jungles of southern Thailand.

This area covered most of the Kra isthmus north of Songkhla. According to the highway official, in the previous month a Thai survey team had been forced to abandon their venture on the first day, having lost one of their vehicles while crossing a swollen river in this area. If the jungles of southern Thailand had proved too challenging for a survey team with comparatively modern four-wheel-drive vehicles, the odds against Noel and I 'pulling it off' were stacked high.

To our advantage however we had favourable weather conditions – we'd planned our journey around the weather, and by choosing February 1st as the departure date, were confident to have missed Thailand's monsoon season. In comparison, the survey team had been operating during the monsoon season, when large tracts of jungle turn into swirling lakes. Significantly, it was almost a week since we'd left Singapore, it hadn't rained and, given the brassy sun, the weather appeared set in our favour.

Krabi, a name that makes you want to scratch, is a tiny place perched on the west side of the Kra isthmus, and 150 miles north-west of Songkhla as the crow flies. The only route to Krabi was through dense jungle. We were aiming to drive from dawn to dusk, and to cover 50 to 75 miles per day, and expected the journey to take about three days.

The arduous terrain meant the Jeep was constantly in four-wheel-drive or low gear, so the fuel needle dropped at an alarming rate. Shortage of fuel, however, wasn't an issue, since we were carrying 23 gallons, which was adequate to cover this stage. We were also confident in our ability to survive in the rainforest for weeks. Our only concern was severe illness; there was no 'on-tap' rescue mission to bail us out. [1]

Several miles out of Songkhla as we headed towards Krabi, the road deteriorated into a rough track and cut through an area of wild coconut palms. We pulled up next to a couple of men splitting the green husk away from the coconuts they'd collected with their machetes and tried to establish the direction to Krabi.

'Krabi this way?' We gave up trying to establish directions after Noel, who'd offered cigarettes and pitched the same question in Cantonese, was presented with a couple of coconuts.

Cigarettes, fish-hooks, sewing-needles and soap - which are taken for granted in the West, served as a currency in these remote villages, and were easily exchanged for food and other commodities.

Shortly after leaving the coconut collectors, the jungle encroached onto the track, where an overhead branch hit the windscreen and lanced through the canvas roof. With the torn canvas tucked over our supplies - it had no other use, the windscreen clipped down onto the engine cover to reduce the chance of it shattering, we were now entirely dependent on the air force goggles for protection.

Noel snapped the compass shut. *'Still on about 330 degrees, Roy. We should be taking a more westerly course. How many miles since leaving Songkhla?'*

'Only about 25.' I checked the mileometer. *'Hope we're on the right bloody track.'*

The driving conditions deteriorated and the Jeep was pushed to its limit as we progressed further into the jungle. On reaching a steep upward incline, we stopped to let the engine cool and noticed that one of the back rear tyres was flat. This was our first but by no means last puncture.

The simple process of changing a tyre requires considerable skill in the jungle where the jack tend to bury itself in the soft earth. The more we cranked the jack, the more it burrowed. Eventually, using the axe and a

On the way to Krabi.

couple of parangs, we made a small log base from nearby saplings, and managed to change the wheel by jacking off it.

When we parted the two halves of the wheel, it was clear the tyre inner tube was mangled beyond repair. [2] It took over an hour to fit the spare, reassemble the wheel, and inflate the tyre with the foot pump. By the time we'd finished, it was too dark to drive, so we searched the immediate area for signs of Communist guerrillas, then set up camp. Having performed this task hundreds of times, the smell of a fry-up began to waft through the jungle within seconds.

Noel forked the sizzling tinned bacon around the pan. *'37 miles, all we've done today, Roy, and that's without negotiating any rivers.'*

'At this rate, it'll take us well over 12 months to get home.' I sprinkled sachets of tea and sugar into the billycan, scraped the black, plaster-like preservative from a couple of 'hundred- year-old eggs,' then passed them to Noel to 'crack' into the pan. [3] Once used to the fishy taste, these antique eggs made ideal supplements to our operational rations. Their

preservative casing ensured they didn't go stale, and they were less prone to breaking.

Nightfall always arrives quickly in the jungle, heralded by an orchestra of insects. Slowly at first, the music opens with a prelude given by a few cicadas, then after several grating skirls, millions join in, until the sound builds up to an ear-piercing crescendo. If on cue, the cicadas usually lower their volume, allowing other insects, frogs and lizards to contribute to the cacophony. It's a unique sound.

Once accustomed to the varying pitches and tones, this orchestra acts as a great lookout post; a sudden, diminishing change of sound usually indicates the arrival of larger mammals; a wild cat or Communist on the prowl. Whatever the beast, once danger has passed, the orchestra invariably resumes its staccato rhythm. We sat well into the night by the soft glow of the stove, listening to this chorus, talking, sipping tea and watching the moon shadows turn the rainforest into an increasingly sinister-looking place.

Making camp just outside Songkhla.

I opened my eyes and stared at the blackness above. Noel was already attending to the stove. We'd slept fully clothed, but ached with cold from being wrapped in damp blankets, and lying on the thin, waterproof ponchos. Condensation showered off the trees soaking me to the skin as I scrambled from beneath my mosquito net to join Noel.

The moisture from our clothes began to evaporate as darkness gave way to daylight while we squatted on the ground with a mug of tea and couple of ration-pack oatmeal biscuits.

'Hope the bastard starts.' I sat in the damp driving seat cleaning my goggles.

'It's a long trek back to Songkhla if it doesn't.' Noel climbed into the passenger seat, his compass close to hand. [4]

I partially opened the choke, then gunned the starter. The damp engine groaned as it turned over, gave a weak 'phut, phut,' then resigned in a halo of blue smoke. Giving the engine a bit more choke, it backfired, coughed out more fumes, then burst into life. We were off.

'Five past six, ready when you are, Roy.' The sun was already gilding the clouds, so we were in for a scorcher, and aiming to drive for 10 hours. In the first two hours, we covered 17 miles, and consumed almost three gallons of petrol as the Jeep slithered along the jungle track in four-wheel-drive, constantly throwing us from the seats.

'Not bad considering we've crawled for much of the way.' I reached for the coffee flask, one of the two we always make at breakfast to see us through the day.

'We're doing all right.' Noel handed me the compass. *'We've been tacking all over the place, but our mean course has kept around 300 degrees.'*

Gazing along the track, to the point where it disappeared into the undergrowth, the ground suggested we were approaching an acute, corkscrew incline. It was impossible to establish our exact location with the large-scale map, but by dead reckoning,[5] we could reasonably assume to be about halfway across the Kra isthmus, 100 miles south of Krabi.

We ascended the incline with great difficulty, but from its peak, the track made an equally acute descent, before coming to an abrupt end. Unprepared for this change in terrain, we lost control of the Jeep, veered through the undergrowth and into a swamp. We didn't waste a second bailing ourselves out. I tied a length of rope around the trunk of a nearby tree and fastened the winch to it, while Noel ran out and hooked the steel cable to the rear of the Jeep. Once everything was in place, and hoping the clove hitches were tied correctly, I worked the ratchet lever and eased the slack out of the cable.

'Noel, keep clear, in case it snaps.' The cable began to take the strain.

'Good winchee – velly strong.' The 'guarantee' from the Arab Street dealer inappropriately sprang to mind as I cranked up the tension on the cable, and gingerly worked the lever until it made the metallic 'click-click' sound, as the pawl engaged the toothed wheel.

'Nothing's happening.' Noel, knee-deep in the swamp, was pushing his shoulder against the back of the Jeep. The cable was now strained to almost breaking point, but the Jeep remained stationary. Carefully, I released the tension.

'It's no good, we'll have to lighten the Jeep. Good bloody winchee.' I cursed, promising to visit the market trader when I returned to Singapore.

After unloading the three full jerry cans, boxes of rations, camping equipment and spare parts, we shovelled most of the mud from around the wheels. There was little hope of rescuing the Jeep if the cable broke, but something had to give. It was now considerably lighter, so we tried again. Tooth-by-tooth, the ratchet was cranked up. Just as it reached the point where I expected the cable to snap, Noel triumphantly brandished the spade.

'Keep it going, Roy.'

Confident the cable wasn't going to snap, I worked the ratchet handle until the Jeep, omitting an acrid smell, dragged clear. The clutch, as we'd anticipated, was slipping, and there was no forward traction. In the hope of making a temporary repair, I crawled under the chassis to give the adjusting screw several turns.

'Hope the bastard lasts until Bangkok.' Noel put the spanners and other tools in the footwell, then wedged the axe and spade behind the passenger seat so they could be instantly grabbed. It was time to move on.

Most of the rivers we'd crossed had been shallow, and by dropping into second gear and driving as slow as possible, to prevent water contaminating the engine, we'd encountered little trouble. However, as we approached the next river, the track disappeared. There was no sign of it reappearing on the opposite bank, which was curtained in vegetation. Since it was unlikely to simply 'end,' we waded through the river, (which

River crossing, Thailand.
'The water lapped dangerously high over the bumper mid-stream.'

had a strong undercurrent and in places was chest high) until we found the remains of the track, an ill-defined slope, in the bank upstream.

Given the depth of the water it was impossible to drive across the river, so our next move was to partially strip down the Jeep, build a raft, and ferry the parts across.[6] Raft building material is prolific in the jungle since there is a variety of low-density, softwood trees, and stout bamboo which grows to over 40 feet. Additionally, we had yards of rope and nylon parachute cord, which was ideal for the lashings, and were experienced in making rafts to ferry our platoons across much wider rivers.

Shortly after we'd started to unload the Jeep, Noel noticed the wheels were no longer touching the water's edge. On closer inspection, we could see thickets of mangrove with long, serrated leaves, trees with stilt-like aerial roots, and mud skippers skating across the silt; we'd hit a tidal river. Immediately abandoning our raft-making plans, we waited for the water to ebb and prepared to drive across the riverbed by removing the fan belt, fixing on the exhaust extention, and changing into shorts, flip-flops, and goggles

Once the ebb slackened, Noel drove the Jeep into the river, while I walked ahead looking for rocks and tree trunks submerged in the silt – many were now exposed. The water lapped dangerously high over the bumper midstream, and the engine was on the brink of stalling. After carefully negotiating the riverbed, we arrived at a sandbar on the far side, close to where the bank stepped down from the track into the river. Noel kept the engine running, occasionally giving it a blast, while I waded over to the exit with the spade and dug away the step. Once the access was clear, Noel released the clutch, letting the Jeep shoot up the slope.

'A close one. Just think if we'd stalled.' Noel fumbled for a cigarette from a battered packet.

'There's even water in the floor pan.' It had been close, all right. The river was over two feet deep, and the cable, too short to reach a strong tree anchor point. If the engine had packed up it would have been impossible to winch the Jeep free.

'Ten to five. We've *been on the way for over ten hours.'* Bars of sunlight from the west angled down through the shadowy jungle. Dusk would be upon us shortly, and we needed to knock off a few more miles.

'Stop about half past, shall we, Roy? That'll give us time to make camp before dark.'

'Yes, roll on five thirty – I'm famished.' The meagre contents we'd eaten

from a couple of 'goody bags' - a few barley sugar sweets and oatmeal biscuits, hadn't satisfied our hunger, so when Noel spotted a stream we checked the immediate area for signs of Communist activity then made camp.

'What do you fancy, Noel?' I picked up a couple of ration tins.

'What about some of that stewed steak, spiced up with curry powder?' Rooting through the two ration boxes for the tinned meat, I realised the black stencilled lettering on all the tins had been rubbed away by the constant vibration of the Jeep. With the tins now unidentifiable, our meal that evening, and indeed many a meal thereafter, was a surprise.

We'd slipped into a good working routine, where each morning, while Noel reloaded the Jeep, I checked it over for damage, topped up with oil, and water and ensured the main petrol tank was full. On this particular morning,when I poked my head under the bonnet, the generator was hanging loose from its brackets – a couple more miles, and it would have fallen off.

Given the favourable weather conditions, we expected to reach Krabi, our next destination which was about 60 miles away by midday. Shivering, I sat behind the wheel as skeins of mist swirled along the ground. When we broke camp, the jungle was still in semi-darkness, chilly, damp, and foreboding. An hour later we arrived at a towering, limestone outcrop where the trees were gnarled and the air pregnant with the sickening smell of decaying vegetation. A dense green vapour swirled over the ground covering the giant fungi and thick velvet moss which grew rampant. Except for the underlying whisper of insects, this mystical landscape was silent. We pulled up to take in the atmosphere.

'The lost world.'

When we stopped for the first changeover of the day, the jaundiced sky had already been prised open by the sun, and the ground mist had disappeared.

'Another scorcher.' Scooping a mug of water from the canvas bucket hooked onto the driving mirror, Noel scanned the terrain for a decent place to take a bearing.

This was the first opportunity we'd had to confirm our position since leaving Songkhla. To our left, the ground was elevated, but not too steep, and there were plenty of saplings and exposed roots, so it was easily climbed. Looking through the latticework of trees from our vantage point, the jungle dropped away into a flat plain then joined the Indian Ocean.

Looking across the Indian Ocean.
'We'd made it across the kra isthmus to the shores of the Indian Ocean.'

Looking north-north-west we could just make out a cluster of islands. Taking their bearings and working on our general course, we were some 25 miles, as the crow flies, south of Krabi. Our route, however, was a twisting jungle track, so the mileage would be significantly more.

'Shouldn't be long now.' Noel pulled on his goggles and released the clutch. An hour and a half later we rattled into Krabi. We'd made it across the Kra isthmus from the Gulf of Thailand to the shores of the Indian Ocean.

We pulled up by a food stall on the seafront and instantly became the 'talk of the town' while enjoying fruit drinks and banana-leaf-wrapped delicacies. Europeans were a novelty, and Noel and I were no exception in our unkempt attire.

'Who speak English?' We prompted the onlookers in the hope of being given directions to Renong.

'I do a little.' A young man stepped forward, nervously putting his hand across his mouth. We complimented him on his excellent English, which seemed to put him at ease. *'Renong, its on the coast.* You go Takua Pa first, long way, 190 kilometres.'

Noel turned against the breeze, clutching the map, and checked the conversion table. *'Make a bloody good kite.'* In addition to being difficult to read when unfolded, these large-scale wall maps seemed to act as a signal for the wind to pick up.

'120 miles. We've eaten, lets go for it, Roy, it's not yet eleven o'clock.'

We made good headway to the coastal settlement of Takua Pa - a string of attap-roofed houses, on the side of a broad river. Within minutes of stopping, the Jeep was engulfed by a group of inquisitive locals. Gesturing with our hands, we managed to explain why we'd arrived in their settlement, then set up camp for the night close to the quay.

Our transport to cross the river to continue to Renong was a rusty barge, waiting to be released from the mud by the next pulse of tide. The only indication that it hadn't been abandoned was a line of coloured washing dancing in the evening breeze above its deck. Just before sunrise the following day, we awoke to the throb of her diesel engine and watched from beneath our mosquito nets as she loomed through the river mist, towards the quay. The 'skipper', who was coiling the mooring line around a bollard was reluctant to commit to a departure time.

'Maybe we leave in one more hour. You American, eh?'

'No, English.' I politely corrected, watching him knot the rope.

'English man good.' His bare feet slapped through the mud as he waded towards us.

'I'm Prem. Me and friend drive ferry.' He flicked a wing of black hair across his forehead.

'Have you English cigarette to spare, please?' Noel offered him an open packet.

'Player's. Very good, thanks. Instead of money for crossing river, you give cigarettes, eh?' Tapping the pocket of his glossy zipper jacket, he fingered out a cigarette from Noel's packet.

'For 20 sticks of Player's I take you over.' Prem quickly came to the point and flicked his lighter into action. *'Eh, you like Ronson lighter? I*

buy from 'Merrycan in Bangkok.' Drawing heavily on his 'stick,' he began to haggle until we agreed to exchange 15 Player's for a river crossing.

Although this vessel wasn't designed to transport vehicles, for a few English cigarettes, and irrespective of the consequences, the 'skipper' was game to carry anything. This was our first introduction to ferry crossing with the Jeep, and we boarded with relative ease since it was close to the quay. At the time we were unaware of the number of ferry crossings our journey would involve, and although we considered this craft inferior, in comparison to its counterparts, it was a world-class vessel.

'River coming deep, not long we go.' I ducked under the line of washing, soggy with overnight dew, and took a closer look at Prem's lighter as he stood by the tiller.

'I pay plenty money to 'Merrycan airman.'

'It's a Japanese fake. You can always tell, they spell 'Ronson' with a 'U'; 'Ronsun.' I indicated the discrepancy of the lettering but failed to convince him he'd been duped.

The ferry moored at a settlement a few yards downstream, where as soon as we'd disembarked, half a dozen coolies burdened with produce destined for Takua Pa and other remote, jungle villages clambered aboard.

Our next destination was Renong, 115 miles to our north. According to Prem, a new road was presently under construction between Renong and Takua Pa. Although it was by no means complete, there was a path bulldozed through the jungle for about a quarter of the way, which would reduce the off-road driving to about 85 miles. Prem tried to define where we'd pick up the trail, with one of his passengers hidden beneath a conical hat.

'This coolie say elephant trail over there go to Renong.' He indicated a clearing along the riverbank. *'It follows river for a short distance, then turn north, and when he work elephant, journey take five day to Renong.'*

Although the disused elephant trail seemed an unlikely starting point, we thanked Prem and headed for the clearing. True to form, the trail hugged the meandering riverbank for a mile, then as it turned north, deteriorated. Most of the wooden bridges that had formerly supported the weight of elephants over streams along the track were now rotten, and the timbers had to be reinforced from surrounding pieces of wood, then secured with parachute cord before we could cross. Shortage of petrol, which reduced the Jeep's overall weight, was now probably to our advantage.

After passing the road construction, the track returned to the jungle, where, without warning, a bird of prey swooped out of the middle distance and smacked into the windscreen. Easing its talons off the glass, it flapped awkwardly overhead, then corkscrewed down into the undergrowth. The bird's unexpected attack was impossible to avoid, and its death, confirmed in a profile of downy feathers across the windscreen, plagued us for days.

Contrary to 'expert' opinion, we survived the Thai jungle, and made it to Renong with a broken rear spring and just teaspoons of petrol to spare. Battling with a flaming wok, the Cantonese cook in the local chop suey house acknowledged our entry with a brief nod.

'Too hot. What you like?' He raked the charcoal embers on the stove then, delighted to hear Noel reply in Cantonese, turned to his native tongue while dishing-up double portions of chow mein.

With the meal over, we celebrated the successful passage through the Thai jungle over a few beers, but by the time we came to leave, we could hardly walk. Amused by the error of our ways, the cook offered a room above the kitchen where we slept in a semi-drunken stupor on the floor. The reality of the surroundings became all too apparent the next morning

Filling up with fuel in Renong.

when we were faced with a communal sink: in this instance a water butt, and open latrines, sizzling with flies.

The route to Bangkok, (where we were hoping to replace the spring), was comparatively less rugged, and frequented with petrol points. The opportunity to take on fuel 'little and often' enabled the weight on the springs to be kept to a minimum. For all the advantages of this main artery, the journey to Bangkok was fraught with reckless, Thai lorry drivers, constantly hounding the back of the Jeep, before forcing us into the gutter as they overtook.

On approaching the coast, we carefully manoeuvred across a series of wooden bridges. Although they were made of strong logs, the distance between the parallel planks was set for wider-tracked vehicles which meant the front and rear left wheels balanced on the planks, while the right, richocheted over the supporting logs.

Within minutes of catching a flash of shiny sea through the palm trees, we entered Chumphon, where we took on a couple of gallons of petrol, then pushed on. We had now crossed the Kra isthmus twice, first east to west, then west to east.

Tracing the palm-fringed coast north to Prachuap Khiri Khan, our main concern now was food, sleep and failing cluth, which had again started to slip. Desperate to reach Bankok before the clutch packed in, we found some cheap accomodation, then spent the afternoon on essential maintenance: the carburettor was stripped, cleaned, and the clutch adjusted to the limit.

Approaching the village of Hua Hin, the dirt road threaded its way through palm trees as it ran parallel with the beach before filtering into an asphalt surface, where a nail punctured one of the back wheels, shredding the inner tube beyond repair.

By noon, we'd traversed through an area of paddy fields approaching Bangkok, where the clutch began to falter as we negotiated dense traffic for the first time. Unable to pull away at traffic lights without enlisting the help of pedestrians or trishaw drivers, we caused mayhem in the centre of the City. After half a dozen 'push starts,' the Jeep collapsed outside Bangkok's luxurious Grand Hotel.

Bed and breakfast at The Grand was well outside our budget, but having 'roughed it' for several days,we were confident the cost would soon be offset against weeks of sleeping rough. The Grand's Swiss manager had other ideas: disregarding we had a change of clothes which were more in keeping with the hotel, and much to the relief of a group of on-looking guests, we were ordered outside.

At the Hotel Metropole, a few hundred yards down the road, we asked the porter to call the manager outside. This tactic worked a treat; we were offered en suite rooms in a newly built annex at the rear of the hotel, and the Chinese manager arranged for the Jeep to be towed away, and repaired by Bangkok's main Jeep agents.

That evening we happened to share a dining table with a middle-aged couple from London.

'Frank Sykes, I'm in wood!' Fortunately, he wasn't a sewage engineer.

'Vera, my wife.'

One of the better bridges in Thailand.

Frank was employed by a company based at Tilbury Docks that imported teak. Combining business with pleasure, he visited Bangkok each year with his wife Vera, who was 'in flowers.'

'It's a perk of the job.' A junky gold bracelet jangled about his wrist as he tapped the side of his nose with a ringed finger. 'Vee and I love it here.'

'It's wonderful. The shops are great, and you can guarantee a decent tan.' Vera fingered an earring, exposing the black roots of her platinum-blonde hair.

'Only spent three hours by the pool this afternoon, and just look how the sun's caught me.' Slipping the spaghetti-like straps off her white cocktail dress, she rubbed the remains of her suntan lotion into lobster-coloured shoulders, then holding a chopstick in each hand, attacked a bowl of noodles.

'We always eat Chinese food with 'sticks.' Frank's failed attempt to retrieve a slice of duck clasped between his chopsticks was all too evident in the sanguine stains on his shirt and tie.

'They don't usually cut it this small.' He picked a slice of duck off his lap and licked his fingers. Vera faired little better with a ravel of egg noodle, tangled around her chopsticks.

'Duck's tasty.' A line of sweet and sour sauce meandered onto Frank's jacket, while he tried to deliver another portion of meat to his mouth. Vera, with overloaded chopsticks and ballooning cheeks, was also still experiencing difficulty.

'Noodles OK, Vee?'

'Went down the wrong way.' Vera managed a quick nod, blanched, and reached for her gin and tonic.

Whoop, whoop, whoop. The paddle fan in the foyer of Bangkok's Burmese Embassy chopped slowly through the hot air, moving it from one part of the room to another. It had no impact on the heat: even a wooden sculpture of the chinthé looked dehydrated.

We handed the document folder to a young military officer.

'Ah! The two men in a Jeep. Our people in Singapore advised you were on the way. My orders are to take you to our senior diplomat Mr Lin. This way, please.'

The journey hinged on these visas. If, at the eleventh hour, the Burmese retracted their offer allowing us to drive through their isolated country, we'd be on our uppers.

'Mr Lin, Mr Dudgeon and Mr Follows.' The officer made the initial introductions, saluted then left the room.

'Take a seat, gentlemen.' There was a plummy edge to Lin's voice. He looked to be in his forties, dressed in a crisp linen suit, and 'old school tie.' A map of Burma covered the wall behind his desk, which was home to several framed photographs of a cricket team.

He opened the folder and scanned our papers. *'Malayan Police! So that's the connection. I see now why our top people in Rangoon approved your visa applications.'* Resting his elbows on the desk, he steepled his fingers. *'As you English say, someone must have pulled a few strings. You are indeed most fortunate.'*

'Thank you, sir.' We could not disguise our relief at hearing his words: we were finally going to receive visas to travel through Burma.

'It's not that cut and dried – don't get too excited.' Lin twirled the signet ring on his little finger. *'Your visas are a special case. My orders are to endorse your passports with a proviso. When you read it, you may wish to change your mind about Jeeping around Burma.'* Taking a pen from the inkstand he wrote *'Permitted to enter Burma by land route at own risk.'* inside our passports.

'See what I mean, about having second thoughts?'

'What does this proviso really signify?' We pressed.

'I do not wish to sound unhelpful, but to put it bluntly, you are entirely on your own. No military vehicles to escort you through dangerous areas, you are not my government's responsibility. Don't expect any official help. I'm sorry, but that's the situation. Think about it, gentlemen.'

The reality of the proviso slowly registered, but it wasn't going to be a deterrent. Lin wasn't surprised.

'Do you expect to arrive home in time for the Test Matches? England are playing the Kiwis this year. Cricket is my favourite game.' He picked up a couple of framed photographs from the table. *'This is my boarding school in England, I went on to become a Cambridge Blue. Those were*

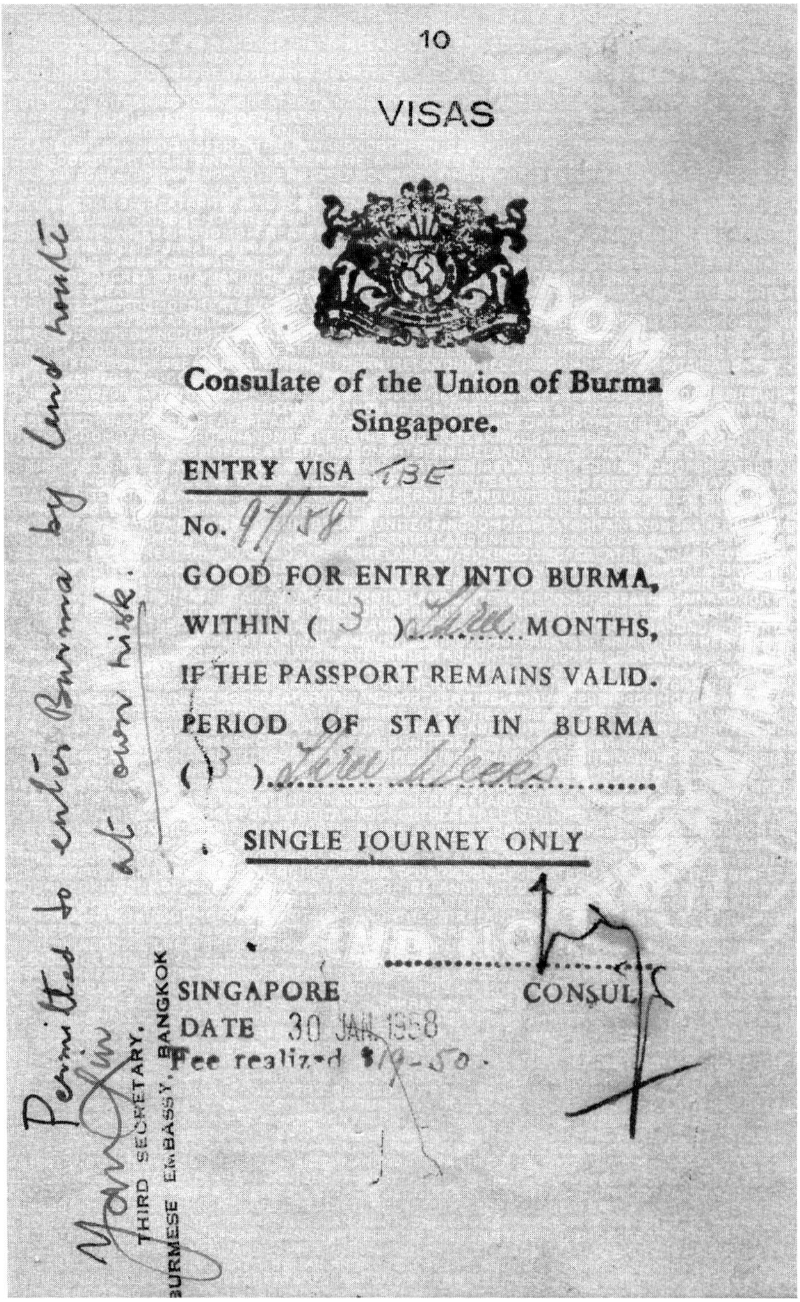
10

VISAS

Consulate of the Union of Burma
Singapore.

ENTRY VISA TBE

No. 97/58

GOOD FOR ENTRY INTO BURMA,
WITHIN (3) Three MONTHS,
IF THE PASSPORT REMAINS VALID.
PERIOD OF STAY IN BURMA
(3) Three Weeks

SINGLE JOURNEY ONLY

SINGAPORE CONSUL
DATE 30 JAN 1958
Fee realized $19-50.

Permitted to enter Burma by land route at own risk.

THIRD SECRETARY,
BURMESE EMBASSY, BANGKOK

The Burmese Visa complete with proviso:
'Permitted to enter Burma by land route at own risk.'

the days. I'm hoping my next assignment will be the Burmese Embassy in London.'

The day before we were due to leave Bangkok, I went down with malaria. I'd dosed myself with medicine from a local herbalist, but its effects were nominal: I could barely walk, think, and certainly couldn't drive. From my experience of previous malaria attacks, I knew this would be short but severe. Confident I'd recover within a couple of days, we kept to our departure date. Noel was prepared to both drive and navigate.

The Jeep's clutch, spring, shock absorber, wheel bearings, brakes, exhaust system, and steering mechanism were now repaired. Prior to heading 215 miles north to Nakhon Sawan, and the Thai-Burmese border, we tested the vehicle through the streets of Bangkok: it seemed like new.

There were three border posts from Thailand into Burma all of which were prone to insurgent activity, and therefore sporadically closed.[7] To save on fuel, and against better advice, we risked taking the shorter, most dangerous route. This meant crossing into Burma at Mae Sot, then on to Kawkareik and the port of Moulmein where we were certain of buying petrol.

My recollection of these two days is vague. I curled up on the passenger seat, where Noel saved me from falling out a number of times by swiftly grabbing my clothes. The side effects of the quinine-based medication brought on involuntary vomiting. The advantage of being in an open vehicle was that I could lean over the side to throw up, however after the vomit had blown back into my face several times, before leaning out to retch, I gave Noel the cue to slow down. On reaching Chainat, I'd taken a turn for the worse, and Noel decided to find a place for me to rest.

Fully clothed and past caring how filthy, or where we were, I collapsed onto a bed. For the rest of that day and all through the night, I lay under my mosquito net, swinging between bouts of shivering, sweating, and hallucination. The last thing I remembered was a pile of flying ants, drawn to their death by a burning coil of mosquito repellent.

When I eventually came to, my head was pounding and I was desperately thirsty - a sign of the fever coming to an end. Lifting a pitcher of water from the bedside table, which tasted old and warm from the morning sun, I cast my eyes towards the threadbare room divide, looking for Noel.

'How are you, Roy? You look much better.'

'Other than feeling as if there's an ice pick through my skull, I'm not too bad.' I pushed away the soiled sheets and, sitting on the edge of the bed, noticed the earth floor, and ornate spittoon in the far corner.

'Where the hell are we?' The bed smelled of urine, and the pillow was stained with tides of sweat and different shades of lipstick. Fortunately I was fully dressed but sensed my clothes were about to become a new-found haven for bed lice.

'Chainat, the back of a mah-jong parlour, we arrived yesterday just before two.' Noel put me in the picture. 'It's about 9.00 a.m. There's no rush, we're only 150 miles from the Burmese frontier.'

Even though I hadn't eaten for nearly two days, I wasn't hungry, but my mouth was acrid, and I was desperate for liquid - a large mug of tea with milk and sugar.

Ducking under a couple of blackened oil lamps, we made our way to the front of the mah-jong parlour, and a table, close to the open frontage where a Chinese man was stuffing fingers of sticky rice into his babies mouth.

'Just tea, Roy?' Noel turned to an elderly lady in a black samfoo standing behind the counter.

'Please, and plenty of it.' I nodded, still dazed, as she hobbled forward, armed with a wet rag to slop over our table.

She returned with a complete, bone-china, doll-sized tea set. I've never understood why the Chinese, who are such masters at cooking, can't make a decent cup of tea. The trouble is these thimble-like cups don't have handles, and while trying to sip the weak black liquid you invariably burn your fingers.

'Too small.' Gesturing for a larger cup, I held the minature vessel between my thumb and forefinger. Pointing to the baby who was still being force-fed sticky rice, she fetched two rice bowls which we filled with tea.

'Hope we're not lowering the tone of the place.' I lifted the bowl to my lips. The tea was a pale whisky colour, sweetened with our own sugar.

Intrigued by the volume of tea we were drinking, she continued to fuss around our table, and after rearranging a few potted plants started to spray an oil-based insect repellent about the room. Common in the East, with the addition of dilute paraffin, this insecticide was sold by unscrupulous traders. As she actively pumped the dispenser, a paraffin haze, impregnated the air, settling the bowls of tea with twinkling stars of oil. If anyone had struck a match, the place would have gone up in flames.

With Noel still at the wheel, we left Chainat for Nakhon Sawan, pulling up next to a couple of American army sergeants - advisers to the Thai military, sitting in a Jeep.

'Limeys! Where you guys from?'

'Singapore – we're on the way to England.'

'Driving to England in that. Holy cow! Did ya hear, Ed?' The sergeant in the passenger seat turned to his friend.

'Sure did, Tex. Only a Limey would attempt such a thing. Say, what's the distance to old England?' Ed chomped on a cigar.

'Not far, only about 12,000 miles from here.' Noel answered in a matter-of-fact way.

'Gee!' You call that not far. Are you guys crazy, or what?'

Intrigued by our journey, Ed and Tex insisted on taking us to a café, where we soon learned, the mountainous frontier region we were proposing to cross was a 'no-go' area, and regular battleground for the Burmese army, launching attacks against the jungle strongholds of the Karen guerrillas.

Tentatively we left Nakhon Sawan, and headed along a desolate, deteriorating road, where hunger pangs, which were satisfied with several bowls of Siamese fish curry, indicated the end of my malaria. Taking to the driving seat for the first time since Bangkok, we continued heading for the remote village of Wangehow where we hoped to pick up the track leading to the Thai-Burmese frontier of Mae Sot. The foreboding spectacle of the Dawana mountains straddled the middle distance.

Endnotes

1 The Jeep's standard 12 gallon [imperial] fuel capacity wouldn't have been adequate.

2 The wheels on a Willys Jeep are split-rim and held together by five nuts and bolts.

3 Eggs preserved in sulphur with a black charcoal coating.

4 When planning the journey, we'd agreed that in the event of being unable to repair the Jeep we'd take it in turns to go and find help.

5 A method of establishing one's position using the distance and direction travelled rather than astronomical observations.

6 An empty Jeep weighs 500lbs (¼ of a US ton). Ref Willys Jeep Manual.

7 See Appendix V. Page 202.

JA 6178

CHAPTER 3

EARTHQUAKE

Ferry crossing - Burma.

CHAPTER 3

EARTHQUAKE

During the night, camped deep in the foothills of the Burmese -Thai frontier, we experienced our first rain since leaving Singapore. The tropical downpour continued until dawn.

The customised lean-to that clipped onto the side of the Jeep made an inadequate shelter. Arrows of rain, driven by hurricane-force winds, stormed horizontally through the open side, soaking us to the bone. As claws of lightning ripped open the clouds and turned the black jungle into flashes of daylight, we had little choice but to sit, wet through, waiting for the dawn. Emerging from our shelter at first light, we found our camp site had been transformed into a quagmire: the Jeep seats, our bedding and equipment were all sodden.

While Noel struggled to light the temperamental stove and organise breakfast, I made a few repairs to the Jeep and filled the two jerry cans from the nearby stream. From the point where we broke camp, the incline of the track spiralled upwards, then hugged the side of the high ground as it contoured through the mountains. It was so narrow in places, a split-second lack of concentration by the driver, or a sudden skid, would have hurled the Jeep off the edge, into the green jaws of the jungle.

From the number of fallen trees, young saplings and undergrowth sprouting up along the trail, nothing had passed this way for months. By mid-morning, a storm was brewing. The sun had failed to break through the brooding sky, and the air was still cool and tacky with moisture.

We didn't have to wait long before a flash of lightning fractured the sky, followed by the beat of thunder. Then the rain began. It was sporadic at first, just a few large drops of water that fell with intent. We braced ourselves as the jungle became increasingly dark, then the hot engine cover began to hiss and steam from the raindrops, which exploded among the trees, and laid waste the undergrowth.

Lashed by the storm, we cowered from the spears of rain, which were now hitting the ground with such force they rebounded. The Jeep's canopy offered no protection, and within seconds the windscreen wipers were bobbling on the screen like a couple of matchsticks trying to hold back the Niagara Falls. In this torrent, cranking a small handle back and forth made no impact. Then, as the water started to cascade down the screen they packed in completely. We were drenched. [1]

We were now unable to control the Jeep, and our vision was so impaired it was like driving through multiple sheets of opaque glass. Hoping the rain wouldn't cause a land-slip, we stopped on the mountain ledge until the torrent ceased. Once the sun dragged itself from behind the clouds we continued worming through jungle passages and tightly packed hills to the summit of a jagged rock from where a panorama of mountainous peaks and valleys stretched into Burma before fading into a purple haze.

Even from this vantage point, trying to fix our position accurately on a 63-miles-to-the-inch wall map of Southeast Asia was impossible. Since entering this inhospitable area, we hadn't crossed any rivers or streams, but somewhere ahead, we knew we'd have to cross the River Moei.

'Please strictly obey this rule.'
'We had no idea what day it was when we passed this sign on the way to Mae Sot, [Maesod] so took a chance.'

On our large-scale map, the Moei was a spidery line, sandwiched between two valleys. On most maps, rivers are not to scale; if they were, according to our map, the Moei would be over a mile wide. Furthermore, maps don't account for fluctuating water levels, and due to the torrential rain, the Moei could have swollen, and prove impossible to cross.

We continued through this rough terrain for another couple of hours, then without warning the track corkscrewed down into a valley, where it became so narrow it took several attempts to edge the Jeep around some of the hairpin bends. A mile or so after levelling out at the bottom, we hit the Moei; it was swollen and fast-flowing, and since there was no alternate route, we had to find a way to cross it.

'Thatched huts Noel, over the other side at two o'clock.'

I'll never forget that moment. We'd just pulled up by the water's edge where I happened to cast my eyes upstream, and look through the trees on the opposite side of the riverbank. There in the middle distance I could just make out a cluster of thatched huts and a group of men quietly tending their water buffalo.

Although initially worried to see two Europeans stranded with a Jeep, we encouraged them to cross the river, which they did with relative ease, then Noel handed out cigarettes as we tried to explain our reason for 'passing by'.

A few sketch maps along with a supply of cigarette 'hand-outs' to gain their trust, soon established where we were travelling to, and why we needed to cross the river.

The remaining villagers came out to watch as one man harnessed a water buffalo to pull the Jeep out of the river and we eased into the water. The stone riverbed provided a firm base, and with the help of couple of villagers wading ahead and the buffalo bringing up the rear, we successfully crossed into Burma.

We arrived at the tiny settlement of Myadadi with no negotiable cash, and as we'd expected, the speckle of shopkeepers hadn't heard of traveller's cheques, so we had no other choice than to barter. We were directed to a small hut with smoke-blackened walls made from bamboo and hammered tin cans.

'Sahib wants food? Only egg and chapatti have.' The bare-chested Indian momentarily stopped slapping dough between his damp palms. A needle-thin cigarette hung from his lips.

'Before, I was many years cha wallah in British Army.' Adjusting the grey dhoti around his waist, he listened with amusement as we offered to exchange several pairs of socks for a plate of egg and chapatti. After some haggling, we traded a few cigarettes and a couple of pairs of socks for chapattis and boiled eggs: if he'd asked, we'd have given him the shirts off our backs.

'Just imagine,' said Noel, as we squatted on the ground, our backs leaning against the Jeep, *'back home, trying to barter socks and cigarettes for tea and biscuits at a roadside café.'*

We pressed on along the mountain track for some forty-five miles, reaching Kawkareik, where we officially checked into Burma, just before nightfall. Surprised that we hadn't been seized by one of the warring factions when crossing the Dawna mountains, the customs official insisted on taking us for a celebratory meal of duck and fried rice.

By day three, we were in need of a bath, so that evening persuaded the inspector at the local police station to put us up in a cell for the night. Regrettably, the adjoining bathroom consisted of a ladle and a couple of Shanghai jars filled with water, and since we weren't adept at this type of bathing, we had to squat on the floor while a couple of officers drenched us.

The following morning both the rear tyres were flat and the foot pump had given up the ghost. We managed to borrow another pump, and stacked everything back into the Jeep once we'd inflated the tyres. Minutes later, one of the back tyres was flat again. Cursing our bad luck, we set about repairing punctures for the third time, then headed west for the coastal town of Moulmein.

The only way to reach Moulmein was to pick up a ferry on the riverbank at Kyondo, then sail down the River Gyaing. We missed the crossing by seconds, so with 24 hours to wait, (there was only one crossing each day) we looked for a place to camp. Just outside Kyondo, our search was called off by a couple of military vehicles carrying armed soldiers who forced us to stop.

In hindsight, we realised they'd suspected we were members of the CIA. one soldier joined Noel in the Jeep after it had been searched, I was ordered into an army wagon, then we were whisked off to their base for interrogation. We'd heard disparaging stories about the Burmese Military, and before being introduced to a senior Gurkha officer, had visions of being held hostage.

'A few weeks ago we attacked a guerrilla camp in the jungle, close to the Thai frontier, at this spot. That's why my men have bought you here.' The Gurkha officer pointed out a red pin on the wall map. *'There were two white mercenaries among the dead, and from documents found on their bodies, we believe they were from the CIA.'*

Noel shot me a meaningful glance. I knew what was going through his mind. [2]

'Gentlemen, I trust you appreciate why you are here – it's dangerous. Instead of camping, you can stay overnight in our fortified compound. I haven't met any Brits in a long time, not since I served with the Indian army during the war, but tell me more about your journey, it sounds interesting. I wonder if my relative knows about you, he's also in the Malay Police Force.' Our concerns about being held hostage instantly dissolved.

With the accommodation sorted, we spent the rest of the day carrying out maintenance work on the Jeep. For the last 100 miles the engine had appeared fuel-starved, so we stripped down and cleaned the carburettor, petrol pump, fuel lines, plugs and points. The leaking cooling system and exhaust was also repaired and the brakes 'bled' and adjusted. We were unable to buy a new windscreen wiper mechanism and managed without for the rest of the journey.

The Gurkha officer agreed to exchange some of our undeclared English currency into rupees, (the traveller's cheques could only be changed at a bank, and the nearest was over 300 miles away in Rangoon) enabling us to buy tickets for the ferry passage to Moulmein and several more gallons of petrol.[3]

To ensure we wouldn't have another 24-hour wait, the following morning we were at the riverbank by 7.00 a.m. The passengers hadn't arrived, and the crew, who wouldn't commit to a departure time, were still at the yawning and scratching stage.

'Jeep go ferry?' Knuckling the sleep out of his eyes, a deck hand reluctantly raised his head.

'Yes, where's the boarding ramp?'

'You provide ramp, we don't make.' Pointing to a heap of old timber, he stifled a yawn.

Watched by an audience of newly arrived passengers, we shouldered lengths of reclaimed wood under the heat of the brutal sun, then began to bridge the gap between the ferry and the riverbank. The parallel timbers were only marginally wider than the Jeep's track, so the finished ramp was far from perfect. Noel inched the Jeep along the ramp while I called out instructions from the ferry. At this point, the thicker timber under the right-hand wheels was supporting the Jeep, while the timber on the left, started to strain under the weight. At the halfway mark, the weaker timber bowed to near-breaking point, as the Jeep listed precariously over. There was no margin for error. Noel carefully eased forward, concentrating on my hand signals until the gap shortened and the Jeep passed the critical point, then rolled onto the deck.

The ferry's departure was determined by the number of awaiting passengers, and not by the time of day. When the last person was squeezed on board around eleven o'clock, she was well-down on her gunwales. A kaleidoscope of characters were scattered across the deck: Indian merchants clutching battered suitcases, Burmese market traders with baskets of fruit, sinewy Chinese balancing sacks of rice and furniture on their bicycles, and shaven-headed monks with saffron coloured robes and serene smiles. We tightened our money belts and stayed close to the Jeep, which was the only vehicle on board. [4]

For the first few hours the river was placid and hemmed in on both sides by jungle as the ferry took the 'scenic route' to Moulmein. Occasionally we stopped at steamy jungle villages, from where narrow planks were pushed onto the deck, and as the ferry listed, people trotting down the planks were replaced by new arrivals trotting up. Moving further downstream, we then joined an estuary, and turbulent undercurrent caused by the mighty River Salween, where the wind blew over from the west, butting the ferry the last couple of miles to Moulmein.[5]

'Ship me somewheres east of Suez, where the best is like the worst,

Where there aren't no Ten Commandments an' a man can raise a thirst,

For the temple-bells are callin' an' it's there I would be -

By the old Moulmein Pagoda, looking lazy at the sea.

On the road to Mandalay

Where the old flotilla lay,'

Mandalay.
Rudyard Kipling.

When Kipling visited Moulmein aboard an ocean-going liner in 1889 it was a backwater. Now it was a bustling port, the third-largest city in Burma, and there wasn't a flying fish in sight.

Deep-sea-going merchantmen and small coasters vied for space at the wharf, and hundreds of coolies, buried under sacks of produce, were commuting up and down gangways. Others ran along the quay pushing handcarts overloaded with tea chests. With the exception of the Indian tally clerks, sitting in little dusty cabins, everyone moved at the double. A Bombay-registered merchantman, secured by thick hawsers and bound for Seattle with a cargo of hardwood and rice, towered above all the other vessels. Possibly one of the last coal burners, she was a battered old freighter, with acrid smoke belching from her blackened chimney, and a white superstructure stuccoed with rust.

From Moulmein, we were aiming to cross the Salween delta to Martaban by ferry, but the ticket clerk grossly inflated the price of the crossing, which meant we didn't have enough rupees to pay; even a couple of dollar bills waved under his nose failed to persuade him to compromise.

'Psst! psst! I hear you speak ferry man. I know boat take you to Martaban.' A bare foot boy, whose eyes slipped about nervously, sidled over to the Jeep as we contemplated our next move.

The ferry was an old craft, along the lines of a dhow with the customary lateen sails. Due to sailing regularly between the Andaman Islands and Burma, with a cargo of loose copra, she was impregnated with the sickly smell of decomposing coconut kernels and infested with flying copra beetles.

The putrid diesel engine used for manoeuvring in and out of ports was aft, below deck, and flooded with bilge water. She was about to leave for Martaban and pick up cargo for the Andaman Islands, and the tenacious-looking skipper, preferring not to sail across the bay empty if there was money to be made on the side, agreed to take us aboard. The ramp we knocked up from pieces of waste dunnage, only just spanned the gap between the ferry and riverbank, so the gradient was particularly steep, but since the skipper was anxious to cast off, we had no time to search for longer spars, and had to risk it.

Slamming the gears into four-wheel-drive, I edged forward until the front wheels touched the ramp, then, guided by Noel, who was on deck, began to crawl up the planks. Without warning, the Jeep listed over as the right plank shot from beneath the wheels. I managed to jump from the driving seat[6] just before the Jeep slipped down between the hull and the quay, then wedged nose-first, inches above the water.

With the help of the skipper and his five-man crew, we quickly tied ropes from the Jeep to a nearby bollard. Once secured, we lowered ourselves down onto the Jeep, reaching first for the survival rucksacks and document pouch, then anything else we could grab. If the vehicle was assigned to a watery grave we could at least continue our journey – walking.

On hearing the commotion, a group of dockers ran over and offered to help. Once they'd tied a thick, hemp rope around the back axle, they took up their positions like a tug-of-war team, while Noel and I tagged on at the back. With one man shouting the orders, we dug in our heels, and dragged the Jeep slowly back onto the wharf.

Other than the radiator grill and engine cover suffering a few dents, and the tubular-steel roof supports being twisted, the Jeep showed little damage, and the engine burst into life after a couple of splutters. Relieved, we handed out cigarettes to the tug-of-war team, drove back up the ramp with relative ease, then spragged the Jeep onto the deck with rope and dunnage.

A melancholic foghorn acknowledged our designated anchorage outside Martaban. Instead of coming alongside the main pier, where we could see passengers disembarking from other ferries, the skipper manoeuvred between the moored vessels, past the jetty into an effluent tributary, where several thatched huts shouldered the water's edge.

'Why didn't you stop at the landing stage?' We cornered the skipper in his wheelhouse.

'You and Jeep illegal cargo. If caught plenty trouble from government. Don't worry, I unload you away from customs man.'

We finally berthed in a stretch of stagnant water adjacent to a railway marshalling yard and a bamboo raft. There was a little hut perched at the back of the raft with a pole full of washing poking through its window and smoke trailing out of its chimney. The size of a tennis court, this vessel was extraordinary, in that it had had been constructed 'up-country' somewhere on the banks of the river Salween, sailed down to the estuary, then towed by a motorised sampan to its present position. It was now waiting to be dismantled, and thereafter the tons of bamboo which had been used to construct it, would be sold on the ready market.

Immediatley after we'd drived off the ferry and into the marshalling yard, the skipper and a couple of his crew, proffered a flimsy excuse for more money. We'd anticipated something like this was afoot when the vessel failed to moor at the main jetty, so quickly sent them skulking back to their boat with some choice insults.

Lorries unloading cargo on the opposite side of the marshalling yard signalled there'd be an access road, but we first had to cross the busy railway sidings. Dropping the gears into four-wheel-drive, we slowly moved into the sidings, then bounced across three sets of railway lines until we were forced to stop by a passing wagon train. Keeping a sharp look out for rolling stock, we then made a 90-degree turn and continued along the adjoining line, in the direction of the lorries.

'Which way out of the sidings? How far to Thaton?' We pulled up alongside one of the vehicles.

'Thaton?' The driver removed a sprig of leaves, a green cheroot, from his mouth and examined the wet, soggy end.

'Long way.' He shrugged, then in broken English, described how to drive out of the sidings.

So far, our accomodation in Burma had been in the safety of police or military establishments, where we'd been safe, and invariably offered a free meal. On approaching Thaton, we planned to attract the attention of the local security forces, and by capitalising on being 'brother police officers,' secure an invitation to stay in the police compound overnight. The plan worked a treat; within seconds of acknowledging the sentry, and feigning to tinker with the engine, an armoured personnel carrier halted alongside, disembarking a detachment of armed police.

'What you do here? The sergeant provoked, while his men prowled around the Jeep.

'Fixing a loose air filter.' Noel answered impertinently. *'Should be okay now.'* He wiped the spanners on a rag.

'No! No! Not what wrong with Jeep.' The sergeant swatted away Noel's reply. '*Why you come Thaton. You American, eh, have you gun – this?'* He patted his automatic.

'We're English. No firearms, drive from Singapore back home.' Unimpressed by our reply, we were driven to Thaton police station; I was bundled into the carrier 'protesting', while Noel was hustled back into the Jeep. Things were going to plan.

'Malay Police! Interesting.' The elderly superintendent scrutinised our documents. He seemed an amicable chap, and had served with the Burmese Police for over thirty years, under three different masters; the British, Japanese and his own people after Burma gained independence in 1948.

'With the Communist uprising in Malaya, you will be only too familiar with the situation in our country.' The sandbags, barbed-wire compound and pockmarks gouged out of the masonry indicated the station had already come under significant fire.

He flicked through our documents. *'All in order. What's your next move?'*

'Find a hotel in town, and if we can't, make camp somewhere – we're used to it.' Noel answered in the hope of scooping a free bed for the night.

'Hotel!' The Superintendent checked his watch. *'There's only a few, and this time of the day they'll be full, and camping is too dangerous. We'll find you room in our bungalow, it's in the compound just over there.'* He pointed through the window. *'My wife and daughters will be more than pleased to meet you. I trust you like Burmese food, and you can put your camp beds on the veranda behind the sandbags.'*

Our plan had backfired. We would have genuinely preferred sleeping in an empty cell or alongside the Jeep in the compound, but it would have been rude to decline his hospitality. Obliged to have dinner with his family, we now had to unpack the Jeep to find our decent clothes, shave and take a bath; luxuries which could have otherwise waited until Rangoon.

That evening we joined the family for supper. His wife and two daughters were in their best silks, jewellery and traditional sandalwood make-up. The food looked so tempting it was impossible to disguise our hunger. There was chicken prepared in coconut milk, crab in ginger, fermented shrimp paste, (which tastes delicious once you've overcome the acrid smell), rice, vegetables, sauces, and fruit.

The superintendent and his wife went out of their way to make us at home. However, their teenage daughters, who didn't speak English, and had never previously met any Europeans, were understandably reserved. After dinner, the ladies moved to an adjacent room, while our host - who quickly dispensed with formalities and insisted we addressed him as 'Joe,' fetched a decanter and three glasses.

'Cheers.' We clinked glasses. A whisky nightcap seemed a perfect end to the day before hitting the sack. Seconds later, my throat was on fire.

'Local hooch, "Earthquake", we call it.' Another measure was splashed into my glass.

After a few mouthfuls I couldn't drink anymore, but when the bottle was empty, Joe disappeared into a side room, returning with two rifles, plus another bottle of "Earthquake" tucked under his arm.

'In case we're attacked. No doubt, you know how to use them.' He handed over some clips of ammunition and two, well-oiled .303 Lee-Enfields. I manipulated the bolt action. The chamber was empty.

' "Earthquake" good.' When our glasses were refilled yet again, my vision became impaired, and the room began to tremble. Noel seemed unaffected. The last thing I remember was my legs crumbling.

'Roy, Roy.' Somewhere in the distance, a voice ricocheted inside my head. *'Come on, wake up, there's been firing.'* It was Noel's warm Lancashire accent.

'Firing. Where?' I lay on the floor holding my head.

The Superintendant's daughters outside Thaton Police Station.
Note the barbed wire security fence.

'It was heavy, north of here.' Silhouetted by the moonlight, Noel stood peering over the wall of sandbags, his rifle close to hand. *'How d'you feel?'*

'Rotten, even my eyelashes hurt.' I forced a joke as my stomach began to churn and the taste of liquid barbed-wire crawled back up my throat. Clamping my lips on a mouthful of bile, I ran to the sandbags, then threw up the "Earthquake" along with most of the evening meal. The relief was instant. Lifting my rifle, I joined Noel in the vigil.

We didn't have to wait long before the firing, which according to Noel was getting closer, broke out again. The thud of Bren guns confirmed it was something serious. After about 15 minutes of sustained gunfire, several explosions lit up the sky, followed by silence.

'Just gone four. Half an hour since we heard anything. I'm going to get my head down for a couple of hours, wake me if we come under fire.' Desperate to return to the land of dreams, I curled up on the floor in my lightweight blanket.

Noel lit a cigarette. *'I'll have this first, then hit the sack.'*

The next morning, we learned from Joe that insurgents had blown up a couple of bridges along the road to Rangoon. Travel was restricted, and we were obliged to stay in Thaton, until the repairs to the bridge had been authorised. Ironically, if the authorisation took more than ten days, our Burmese visas would expire, and 'Superintendent Joe' would be obliged to arrest us!

Later that day we received news that the railway line hadn't been sabotaged. The stationmaster arranged for us to pick up a freight train in Thaton which would take us the 60 miles to Sittang, (from where we planned to pick up the road leading to Rangoon).

We didn't have enough rupees to pay for the train journey so, set up shop on the pavement near the police compound. With a selection of socks and soap on display, we had an audience of potential buyers within minutes.

'How much you give?' I dangled a pair of grey woollen socks in front of an elderly man, who, like most of the gathering crowd, was barefoot. *'British Army – new, clean.'* I assured.

'Which one left foot?' When we explained they could be worn on either foot he immediately began to haggle for the best price.

15 pairs of socks were sold in the first half-hour. Scented toilet soap, a rare commodity in Burma was next to go on sale. The ladies cooed with delight as they inhaled the fragrance; more importantly, they didn't even haggle over our asking price, and we sold the lot.

When we came to sell the unmarked tins of food, most of which contained pork, or other meat derivatives, we assured the contents were 'vegetarian' and hoped to be well out of town before the cans were opened.[7] Finally, with our 'shop' in full swing, and the temptation to make a quick buck too good to miss, we auctioned off a part-bottle of Scotch.

The flatcar was pulled by an old steam locomotive, and included ten open wagons, all in disrepair, carrying an assortment of freight. The ironwork on all the wheels was rusty, and the wooden flooring decayed. Furthermore, the axle boxes were empty of grease, and from the weeds growing between the tracks it was obvious the wagon had been stationary for years.

While the railway staff lolled about in the shade, we worked against the clock, hauling bulks of timber to make a ramp. Once it was complete, we drove the Jeep onto the deck, then using our own rope, tied it down before the one o'clock deadline.

A small, delicate man with an oversized peaked cap balancing on his ears, a flag in one hand, and a tin whistle in the other, directed the train along the track, in line with the Jeep.

While 'Big Hat' was preoccupied jotting details in his notebook, we scrambled under the flatcar, eased between the buffers to 'hook up' and tried to take the slack out of the coupling by adjusting the seized up bottle-screw.

'Would you happen to be the guard?' Emerging from beneath the wheels, we approached 'Big Hat.'

'Guard!.' The hat wobbled. *'I'm the Assistant Station Master of Thaton.'* His chest puffed out in rebuke as we raised our eyebrows in mock surprise.

'There is no guard on this train, just a driver and fireman.' He disclosed, tilting his head back to get a better view. Then, with a theatrical flourish, he took out his pocket watch. *'One thirty-seven precisely. You should be in Sittang by four fifteen.'* He blasted the whistle, and sliced through the air with his green flag.

No one checked to see if we'd coupled, or secured the Jeep up to the flatcar correctly. There was no guard on board or safety regulations in place. Burma's railway had gone to the dogs, and we could only hope the flatcar remained intact until we reached Sittang.

With smoke and steam thundering from its chimney, the wheels of the locomotive began to turn, then as the flatcar wrenched along the track, we were sent flying off our feet, while the Jeep catapulted within the constraints of its bindings.

Once the engine picked up speed and settled into a rhythm, the jolting gradually stopped. After an initital steady run, it squealed to a halt, and thereafter moved sporadically along the line, stopping at unscheduled places in the middle of dense jungle or paddy field landscapes, where we walked the short distance up to the engine to chat with the driver – it was that sort of railway.

The Jeep took up most of the space on the flatcar, which made it difficult to sit. To move around, we held onto the ropes securing the Jeep, and carefully inched our way along the outer edge, keeping our eyes open for overhanging branches obstructing the track.

The flatcar was totally exposed to the sun, so when we reached Sittang (and disembarked using a couple of sleepers we'd concealed under the Jeep), we were both feeling the effects of over two hours' involuntary sunbathing. We'd also had acute diarrhoea for the last couple of days, and as there were no toilets on board, we'd had to lower our shorts, hang onto the Jeep's bindings and squat over the side. Much to my embarrassment, on one of these occasions, the flatcar slowed down as we passed through a station of awaiting passengers.

Shortly after disembarking from the flatcar, we'd boarded another ferry with the sleepers, and having crossed the Sittang River, tucked into a bowl of soup in a tin-roofed shack with bamboo chairs.

'Rangoon far away, about 100 miles, no good road, many miles of dried paddy-field.'

The waiter fished for more debris in the bottomless pit of his soup tureen while explaining, in the most graphic detail, the 'scenic route' to our next destination, Rangoon. By the time he'd finished, our heads were spinning. Too late to find a place to camp, we pressed on into the night, then dossed down by the Jeep when we were simply too tired to continue.

The overhead dust clouds created as we drove through the vast, arid landscape, outside Sittang, was so intense we had to wear goggles. The ground, having been baked all day retained its heat even when the sun began to slip below the horizon, and as we penetrated further into this hot dustbowl, the cart track gradually disappeared leaving the Jeep floundering up to its axles in a sandy, warm talc. Slamming the vehicle into four-wheel-drive, we continued for over 20 miles through this rough terrain.

With the onset of twilight, we joined a loose-gravelled road. This was an ideal opportunity to disengage from four-wheel-drive, but the transmission remained locked, which meant we were consuming excess fuel. Our progress was now impeded by a combination of ineffective brakes, lack of lights, plus a leaking cooling system, which needed constant replenishing from our diminishing water supply.

'The bloody gear box has gone.' I depressed the clutch, and manipulated the gear levers. Surprisingly, the transmission gave its usual soft murmur, and as I carefully went through 'the box' again, the gears disengaged. The leaking cooling system, which was partially stemmed with adhesive plaster, and faulty gearbox saw us to Rangoon.

Dodging pedestrians and trishaws, we headed towards the Sule Pagoda with its golden spire,[8] then along the Monkey Point Road. Here the barren shops with blinking neon slogans, the lack of hotels, and pavements flecked with beggars and blood-red betel nut,[9] confirmed the extent of Burma's stringent isolation policy.

Replenished with a few snacks from a food stall - we'd earlier wolfed down a tin of cold baked beans to stave off our hunger, that evening we joined Rangoon's low-life in a room with an extraordinary view.

'Welcome, gentlemen. Do you wish for communal loom or plivate?' Noel negotiated the room price in Cantonese and English.

'Too late, gentlemen, only number nine left. Very lucky number. Very lucky room – clean with a nice view. Please this way.'

Room nine, containing a couple of charpoys[10] and a spitoon, was accessed via the 'communal room' where men with carmine-stained mouths, the distinct trademark from chewing betel nut, festered in a drug-introduced stupor.

'Sh sh! Lookey lookey.' Pressing an eye against a concealed hole drilled through one of the adjoining walls, we were invited to take a look.

'See girls and mans jig-jig. Ah! Sleep now, before I see plenty jiggy-jig.' Room nine was special, but not in the way we'd envisaged; it was primarily used for spying on the prostitutes and their unsuspecting clients.

The next morning, Noel sat shivering on his charpoy, and looked in a bad way. It was time to move on. Less than an hour later we booked into The Strand. Formerly one of the world's most prestigious hotels, was sadly in decline. The white, stuccoed walls were flecked with black lichen, and the chauffeur-driven limousines that formerly graced the entrance had been replaced with battered taxis and trishaws. Inside, the ornate ceilings, hardwood panelling, opulent drapes, and carpets had all deteriorated – even the potted palms were drooping. A couple of paddle fans, covered with a filigree of spiders' webs momentarily disturbed the sultry air.

While Noel tried to sleep, I took the opportunity to telephone and thank Mr Prakasam, the Special Branch Officer in the Burmese Police who'd been instrumental in arranging our Burmese visas. On hearing of Noel's condition, Prakasam insisted on calling by the hotel.

'I was informed last night you were in town. Unheard of these days, two Englishmen driving around Rangoon. Where's your colleague?' Removing his Panama, he took a brief look at Noel, and before we'd had a chance to buy him a drink, rang the local doctor.

Noel was diagnosed, and given medication for dengue fever.[11] A few days later, when Prakasam returned to the hotel with information on routes to India, Noel had almost recovered, and keen to take on the challenge of the infamous Ledo Road.

'I suggest you think again about driving the length of the Ledo Road. The terrain along this north-east route to Ledo in India is impossible.' Prakasam cautioned, running a finger around the inside of his olive-green cravat as we studied the few spidery lines of the map fanning out from Mandalay. *'Gieves and Hawkes,'* he smiled, seeing me eye his neckwear. *'At the time I was on a course in England – Scotland Yard.'* For an Anglo-Burmese, he was more English than the English.

Against better advice, we decided to take the more northerly route to India. This included driving along two fascinating arteries: part of the Burma Road, plus the complete, 207-mile length of the Ledo Road. Between Lashio and Ledo, a distance of some 600 miles, we knew there were no petrol outlets. The only advantage of this route was its relative lack of river crossings; the Irrawaddy at Myitkyina was our main concern.

The map on page 82 shows the two roads, plus the route taken from Lashio to Ledo. In its entirety, the Burma Road covers 750 miles from Lashio in Burma, and heads east to Kunming in China. With the Japanese in occupation of Chinese coasts, the Burma Road was one of China's major links and means of transporting supplies during the Second World War. The Burma Road is in fact little more than a track, hand-built by

THE JOHORE CONTINGENT POLICE H.Q.,
BUKIT SENYUM,
JOHORE BAHRU.

21 January, 1958

Dear Dudgeon,

With reference to your difficulties over a Burmese visa, the Director Special Branch, got Mr Thom to write to a personal friend of his, Mr B.S. Prakasam, Deputy Superintendent of Police, Police Headquarters, Rangoon, requesting him to do what he could on behalf of yourself and Follows.

The Director informed me that he did not have any direct liaison with Special Branch, Burma, nor did he personally know the Head of the Burmese Special Branch - hence Mr Thom's letter.

I suggest that if you do have the chance of meeting Prakasam, and have been successful in the visa question, that you thank him for his help, whether or not he actually achieved anything on your behalf.

Yours sincerely

(A.J.W. Slater)
Chief Police Officer
Johore

Police Lieut N.B. Dudgeon,
Police Headquarters,
Johore Bahru.

Letter from Chief of Police, Johore, regarding Burmese visa difficulties.

150,000 Chinese labourers, thousands of whom died during its construction. The Burma Road had remained closed since Burma gained independence in 1948. Thereafer it fell into disrepair. As far as we understood, we were the first people to venture down this forgotten artery since its closure.

The Ledo Road is one of the greatest, but least-recognised engineering feats of the Second World War. Much of its 207-mile route to Ledo, a speck in the northeast corner of India, is uncharted. In 1942, under the command of General 'Vinegar Joe' Stilwell, 28,000 American military personnel, and 35,000 native workers laboured for over two years on the Ledo project. Hacking a military supply route through the Burmese Jungle to Ledo cost hundreds of lives. In addition to those struck down by accidents or disease, many were killed by Japanese snipers.

The Ledo Road was used for seven months up until September 1945 when the Japanese surrendered and hostilities ceased. Thereafter it was abandoned, and reclaimed by the jungle. Winston Churchill tersely predicted the Ledo Road project would be, *'An immense, laborious task, unlikely to be finished until the need for it has passed.'*

With the route sorted, we walked along the Monkey Point Road to the turtle pool in the grounds of the Boatyatung Pagoda. *'Journeys free of mishap and danger'* are guaranteed to all visitors who buy little packets of 'turtle treats' from the enterprising keeper. In light of the journey ahead, we bought a packet of treats and headed for the feeding bay.

Four days later, the Jeep was ready, and Noel had recovered. We left Rangoon and headed north for 'The Golden City' of Mandalay, sleeping en-route in a police post at Kyaukse. We entered Mandalay City from the south, past the main railway station and a string of ponies harnessed to brightly painted 'taxi traps' then joined the Moat Road shouldering Mandalay Fort,[12] which formerly housed the Royal Palace. Never mind the *'wind in the palm trees'* – there wasn't even a soft breeze to deflect the molten heat.

'For the wind is in the palm-trees,and the temple-bells they say:
"Come you back you British soldier; come you back to Mandalay!"

Mandalay.
Rudyard Kipling

Confused by the unfamiliar road signs, we passed every pagoda in Mandalay, before picking up the Road to Maymo which included some 22 hairpin bends.[13] At 3,550 feet above sea level, in the Colonial days,

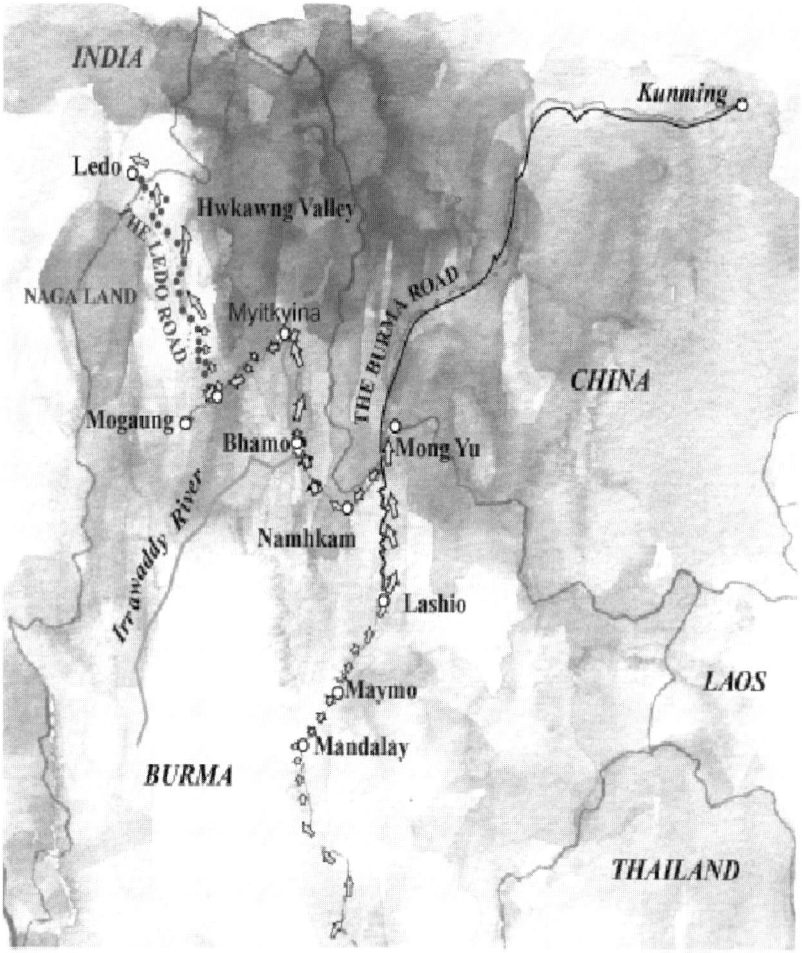

The Burma & The Ledo Roads

The Burma Road	~~~~	From Lashio [Burma] to Kunming [China}.
The Ledo Road	• • • • •	Track 70 miles west of Myitkyina [Burma] to Ledo [India].
Route	⇨ ⇨ ⇨ ⇨	

The sketch map above shows the route taken from Lashio in Burma to Ledo in India. Given the severe conditions, particularly along the Ledo Road, the Jeep performed remarkably well.

On the road to Mandalay.

Buffalo or bike - transport in Mandalay.

Maymo was the favoured place for the British to escape from the oppressive heat of the Burmese plains.[14] We stopped to take in the panorama, and bought a punnet of strawberries. There were also vendors selling locust kebabs, and although we're not that fussy about what we eat, this time we kept to the fruit.

Leaving Maymo for Hsipaw, we carefully negotiated the loose-gravelled road spiralling down into the Goteik Gorge. The monumental Goteik Viaduct, supported by a latticework of steel girders, spanned the gorge to our left with its defiant legs planted between the rocks.[15]

On reaching Hsipaw, where semi-naked infants and mangy dogs squatted with impunity over open-drains, a toffee-coloured trishaw driver, realising we were looking for somewhere to stay, thrust his head inside the Jeep, and introduced himself as 'Charlie.'

Charlie's knowledge of the English language extended to some swear words and military jargon picked up during his time as a 'dogsbody' with the British army in Burma. In return for three Player's cigarettes, Charlie took us to the Public Works Department (PWD) rest house[16] where we were greeted by a caretaker in Mao-style dress, who viewed life from a behind a pair of studious-looking spectacles.

'No one seeks accommodation here now; I can't recall the last time, it's just too dangerous for people to venture this way. Colonial administrators used to stay here while inspecting the area, but since Burma gained independence from Britain in 1948, there's only been a few Burmese visitors. The place is in need of urgent repair work, but the PWD don't seem to care.'

A sickly smell of dry rot took confirmed his words when we stepped through the door. From the background hum and patina of dust, the building was clearly infested with termites, feasting on the uprights, rafters, and furniture.

Brushing away years of debris from a decorative plate, my thoughts catapulted to my home in Staffordshire, synonymous with Wedgwood and Royal Doulton: for a moment I was driving the Jeep along the A34 approaching Stoke-on-Trent.

'The bedrooms are the same.' I sprang back to Burma as the caretaker's voice concluded my daydream. That evening, to limit the chance of infestation, we slept on the floor.

Endnotes.

[1] Jeep windscreen wipers are unique in that they are operated manually, by a handle attached to the wiper arm. The windscreen wipers on our Jeep had been automated (possibly when the Jeep was used by the army), but the electric motor had packed in.

[2] Shortly after one of his successful operations, Special Branch introduced Noel to a member of the CIA. Impressed with Noel's undercover work, the CIA offer Noel a posting, along with a couple more chaps to operate in Burma with a US-backed guerrilla force. With the planning of the overland journey being so far advanced, Noel decided against pursuing the matter further.

[3] So far we'd been unable to buy petrol in Burma, but the long-range fuel tanks, provided sufficient fuel to take us to Moulmein,where we'd been advised fuel would be available.

[4] Any male over the age of eighteen may enter into this religious sect regardless of his previous personal or professional status including criminal convictions.

[5] The source of the River Salween is over 2,000 miles away in Tibet.

[6] Jeeps do not have doors, which on this occasion proved to be a great advantage.

[7] Most Burmese are Buddhists and, in consequence, vegetarian.

[8] The Sule Pagoda has served as the focal point for Rangoon's religious activities for centuries. During the mid-19th century, when the British developed Rangoon's grid-style street system - a mini New York, but with trishaws and temples, the Pagoda was established as the 'hub' of the city.

[9] A predominantly masculine pursuit in southeast Asia and India, chewing betel nut (which is believed to be a digestive, stimulant and narcotic), is almost an art form. A mixture of betel nut, the seed of the betel palm, lime, tobacco, cloves and betel leaves is made into a small quid, then popped into the mouth. Although there is an 'etiquette' regarding how to discard the quid without causing offense, the expectorated betel nut littering the streets is believed to be one of the main causes of tuberculosis.

[10] A bedstead made from woven hemp.

[11] Dengue is more commonly known as 'Breakbone Fever' since one of the symptoms is severely aching bones. Similar to malaria, this acute viral disease is transmitted by the mosquito. The micro-sized sandfly, which can pass through a mosquito net, is also believed to transmit dengue.

[12] The Fort formed a perfect square, with the moat, outer walls, and four roads facing the four cardinal directions. In March 1945 British troops assaulted the stronghold, which was being defended by the Japanese. However, the main palace, which was primarily constructed from teak, had been reduced to ashes, and only the moat and outer walls remained intact.

[13] *The Motor Roads of Burma*, The Burma Oil Co. Ltd. Rangoon Gazette Ltd. 1948 [Publisher] pp.37–39.

[14] 'Maymo' is a distortion of 'Colonel May,' the British army officer, who selected the site for a hill station because of its bracing climate and proximity to Mandalay. Maymo's climate is ideal for growing strawberries,which along with more exotic specialities such as fried locusts, provide a main source of income for the local vendors.

[15] When the Goteik Viaduct was built in 1903, it was considered a masterpiece of engineering. The transort of raw materials to this remote area was also a remarkable achievement.

[16] The PWD was run by the government to oversee roads, railways etc. The PWD houses - usually bungalows, were for use by staff inspecting the area.

CHAPTER 4

UNCHARTED HELL

The Ledo Road.
'The boulders which studded the partially dried-up riverbed had to be removed by hand.'

CHAPTER 4

UNCHARTED HELL

The Burmese town of Lashio, the capital of the Northern Shan states, was buzzing with activity. Proud-looking Shans had travelled down from the hills to trade. Thai goldsmiths were fashioning precious metals using primitive tools passed on from generation to generation. Indian and Chinese traders selling jade and silk rubbed shoulders with humble peasants, just as their forefathers had done in the days of Marco Polo.

Tempted by the smell of cooking, we pulled up next to a bar and stationary mule train. The muleteer's leathery face was steeped in history; was he returning to his settlement in the hills, or smuggling contraband over the mountains, back into China? There was a distinct air of apprehension in Lashio: not the wild west, but the wild east.

When we entered the bar, several pairs of eyes swivelled our way, and as the waiter flicked a rag over the table in a futile attempt to disperse the lingering flies, the chattering stopped. Feeling distinctly uneasy, we drank several bowls of goat broth, then made a quick exit.

Lashio was the last place before reaching Ledo, where petrol was available. A teenage boy directed us to a shop with a hand-written sign that read 'Burma Oil Company' nailed above the door. There wasn't a petrol pump in sight.

'You need help?' The mechanic popped his head from behind a rusty truck, flicked off the radio, and slid his eyes over the Pirelli calendar on the adjacent wall. The skeletal remains of fan belts, gear levers and gaskets littered the earth floor.

Explaining our plight, we followed the mechanic through the shop, into a courtyard, where rows of 5-gallon petrol canisters lay stacked beneath a bamboo shelter. There was no sign of a fire extinguisher, water or sand: if the place had caught fire, the whole of Lashio would have gone up in smoke. The mechanic couldn't believe his ears when we asked for a 40-gallon fill-up, so we had to show him the long-range fuel tanks to convince him we hadn't made a miscalculation.[1]

The petrol canisters didn't have replaceable lids, so we had to puncture the top with a knife, then carefully decant the liquid using a funnel. This was an almost impossible task, which left us soaked in fuel, and provided a great source of entertainment to the cheroot-smoking onlookers.

To ensure we wouldn't run out of fuel, the Jeep's petrol consumption had to average twelve miles per gallon. The critical, but unknown factor was how often the Jeep would be in four-wheel-drive, which makes the engine guzzle fuel at eight miles a gallon. Additionally, if we were unable to disengage from four-wheel-drive, we'd be guaranteed to run short.

Dangerously overloaded with fuel, we pulled up at Lashio's check point with one container tied to the back of the Jeep and the other balanced between my knees in the passenger seat.

'No one is allowed to proceed beyond Lashio without a military escort, it's too dangerous.' Checkpoint Charlie sawed his Adam's apple with the edge of his hand. We hadn't anticipated a police checkpoint on the outskirts of Lashio.

'But we have permission.'

'No. Give me papers – passports, visas.' Desperate to exert authority, the belligerent cop cut Noel short, leafed through the documents and slapped his palm for us to 'chop, chop.' Slowly I reached into the Jeep for the other folder, which was quickly wrenched from my hand.

'Why you get this special visa? You pay?

'We just happen to know your head of Special Branch.[2] Noel retorted.

Returning our documents, he tapped the Jeep's engine cover with the nozzle of his automatic, signalling for us to go.

120 miles from Lashio, the desolate Burma Road sliced through the mountains and the border with Red China, as it headed east to Kunming. Somewhere close to the Burmese-Chinese border post, which wasn't even a pinprick on our map, we had to leave this corpse of a road and head north to the Burmese village of Mong Yu, which butts onto China. If we strayed over the red line into China, we would be liable for causing diplomatic chaos between London and Peking.

'Mong Yu can't be far now.' We were in the no man's land of the ill-defined frontier region of Burma and China. A group of peasants - the only people we'd seen since Lashio, worked the paddy-field landscape. Just minutes later, we reached Mong Yu, a cluster of huts improvised from rags and mud. Although not on our planned route, we were keen to catch a glimpse of the red flag, so edged along the Burma Road to the

The Burma Road.

The Burma Road approaching Mong Yu.

Above: Mong Yu.
Below: Villagers look on.

Chinese border post, then to avoid the Communist guards, reversed back into Burma. The torrential rain and stone road between Mong Yu and Myitkyina presented some of the worst driving conditions throughout the journey: it took two days to cover 300 miles.

Nearly all of our rupees had now been spent on fuel in Lashio, so to pay for a mechanic to repair the broken spring,[3] plus a room in Myitkyina's only guest house, (weather conditions were too severe to sleep next to the Jeep), we sold some of our tropical jungle greens. The money raised still left us with a tight cash-flow, and when the owner of the guest house advised bedding, mosquito nets, mattresses and even oil lamps, were an additional cost, we tried to call his bluff by suggesting we used our own.

'You supply, also more money.'

'And how much for pissing in the communal trough?' We taunted.

'Pissing flee. Bathloom extra.'

That evening, we struck up a conversation with a Mr Brang; a Kachin chief accompanied by two bodyguards with ugly-looking knives planted in their belts. Brang spoke excellent English, and as the evening wore on, revealed an impressive list of 'connections,' inluding a former English, cabinet minister. Although his political associations seemed to tally up, it was only when he pulled a lump of jade out of a leather bag, that we believed he owned a jade mine. This fine green mineral was destined for Hong Kong, and guaranteed to swell his bank account.

Having warned us about the Naga Headhunters whose disputed territory touches on parts of the Ledo Road, Brang arranged for us to meet his friend, Captain Muang, a former army officer in the Burmese Engineers, who'd worked on 'The Road.'

With the approach of the Ledo Road imminent, we'd left nothing to chance. The Jeep and contents of our survival rucksacks had been thoroughly checked, water bottles refilled, and the windscreen secured onto the engine cover. Our only concern was the handbrake, which owing to a lack of spares was still ineffective. We headed for the Captain's shop.

A striking figure in his late fifties, Captain Muang readily dismissed the Ledo Road as *'a costly mule track stamped out of the jungle'.* Since retiring, Muang had invested in several cycle shops in northern Burma. His immaculate suit and manicured hands, confirmed he hadn't touched an oily rag or puncture for years.

He spread our wall map out on the desk and studied it with military precision, tracing a broken red capillary line with the tip of his pencil heading west from Myitkyina towards Mogaung, then due north.

'Hakawng Valley. Uncharted hell, and rife with malaria.'[4] His manicured fingers drummed the spot. *'The locked valley is packed with rivers and streams. If there's a downpour you'll be trapped for weeks – we were in the 1940s.'*

'Hell's Gate, Pangsu Pass, Shing.' We listened intently as he drew a sketch map detailing where to pick up the source of the Ledo Road, plus geographical places along its route, none of which were on our large-scale map.

'The last time I was on The Road was back in 1946, just before it closed. It was an impossible place then, and since it's been out of use for so long it's probably even more treacherous.' He shook his head. *'Good luck.'*

12 miles west of Myitkyina, we pulled up next to a converted bridge pontoon on the deserted banks of the thundering Irrawaddy. Operated by a system of pulleys attached to a wire rope spanning some 400 yards across the river, this rusty vessel had clearly not been used for some time. Eager to cast off, we loaded the Jeep with a pair of ramps from the pontoon, then sorted out the pulley mechanism. Within minutes, the cables started to groan as the current pushed us downstream.

Noel and I had respectively served in the Royal Marines and Merchant Navy, but were complete novices with ferry craft, so it was more by luck than skill that we crossed the Irrawaddy and beached without mishap. Our only setback now was a missing kit bag containing spare towels, winter clothes and blankets. The nylon cord used to secure this vital piece of equipment to the back of the Jeep had been cut – possibly while we were inside Captain Muang's shop.

On Muang's sketch map, the start of the Ledo Road was an overgrown track, a few miles past a small wooden bridge crossing a tributary of the Irrawaddy 70 miles west of Myitkyina. We knew it would be difficult to locate since in addition to being overgrown, it was no longer recognised by government authorities, and therefore didn't qualify for signposts.

Having salvaged a couple of decent planks from the rotten bridge, we made a parallel track for the Jeep, tentatively crossed the bridge, where we spotted a Chinese man, knee-deep in mud, tending his water buffalo. Noel managed to glean from him the exact point, a couple of rusty oil drums, where we'd pick up the start of the Ledo Road. It was purely by

Above: Rafts on the Irrawaddy.
Below: Crossing the upper reaches of the Irrawaddy, west of Myitkyina.

luck, we caught sight of the oil drums adjacent to an overgrown track. Edging past them, the track narrowed and pushed its way through secondary jungle. We were now on the Ledo Road. Within ten minutes, a fine mist blurred our immediate vision like a grey stain. The trees, which were bearded in moss, became significantly taller, the canopy thickened, and the vegetation encroached across the track as we merged into primary jungle.[5]

Stitches of lightning ricocheted across the horizon as we corkscrewed through the undergrowth. It was only a short, intense shower, sufficient to transform the ascending track into a quagmire, and make each mile seem like ten. On reaching the summit, the steep angle of descent almost threw us onto the engine cover. Looking down to the left, the ground fell sharply towards a river, while over to the right, the gradient towered so abruptly it would have been impossible to climb without ropes.

'No brakes. Noel! Noel!' Frantically, I pumped the break pedal as we careered down the incline, then snatched the handbrake – a temporary relief as the overloaded Jeep slowed down. Seconds later the control slackened in my hand.

'The bastard cable's snapped.' I grappled with the steering wheel until the track flattened out, bringing us to a natural halt.

When Noel checked the brake-fluid reservoir our worst fears were confirmed: it was empty. The underside of the Jeep which was enrusted in mud, made it impossible to find the leak in the braking system. The handbrake was also beyond our skills to repair. We'd been on the Ledo Road for less than 20 miles and were already in serious trouble.

Anticipating the brakes were likely to fail again, we took a gamble, replenished the brake fluid, and continued pushing through the vegetation in low gear. Minutes later, when making an emergency stop to avoid a thicket of saplings, we were ejected from our seats, as the brake pedal hit the floor, and the Jeep careered through the undergrowth into a fallen tree trunk.

Bruised and shaken, we sat looking at the Jeep leaning over against the tree, with steam billowing from the engine and the silencer hanging off. There was equipment all over the ground and a heady smell of petrol in the air.

'Christ, Roy, hope the whisky bottle's survived.' Noel, too shaken for a cigarette, countered a smile as we apprehensively started to check the damage.

The Ledo Road.

A punctured top hose (not a damaged radiator, as we'd initially assumed), had caused the steam, and fortunately we had a spare. The exhaust, which had almost ripped off, was relatively easy to secure with light gauge wire, and the battered bodywork was incidental. The brakes were our main concern: brake fluid had been dripping from the left, rear-wheel brake housing, and when we inspected the brake assembly, the rubber sealing ring,an integral part of the slave cylinder, had perished.

'It never rains, but it pisses down.' I toyed with the mangled seal in my palm.

This innocuous piece of rubber *could* be responsible for our failure to complete the journey; we didn't have a spare, so it was essential to devise a way to replace it. There was a slim chance of blanking off the fluid supply to the offending slave cylinder, (leaving the Jeep with effective brakes to just three wheels). Improvisation was the order of the day; we uncoupled the fluid supply line to the faulty brake assembly, packed a wad of chewing gum around a one-inch nail, then forced the shank down inside the pipe. With more chewing gum around the head of the nail, which we prised from the side of the wooden toolbox, we re-coupled the brake pipe, then 'bled' the system. Although we had to drive with caution, thanks to the chewing gum and a spot of ingenuity, the 'blanking off' was successful.

Captain Muang's *'uncharted hell'* rang true when we hit a partially dried-up riverbed studded with boulders washed down from the mountain. The boulders, which were too large to drive over, had to be cleared by hand before crossing to the other side. That night, we set up camp adjacent to an American military pick-up, which we stumbled across near the riverbed. Smothered in vines and creepers, the rusty truck only revealed its true identity after we'd hacked the foliage away from its carcass; undoubtedly it was one of the many vehicles which failed to make it down the Ledo Road in 1945.

Plagued by low fuel levels, and unable to define exactly how far we were from the Indian frontier village of Ledo, we were up before first light checking the brakes and fuel tanks. It was now no longer a question of having sufficient fuel to see us to the Indian frontier, but *how* many miles before we ran out.

The dense jungle canopy now followed a corkscrew trail that ascended steep ridges then plunged into shadowy, green valleys. The terrain was now so congealed with mud, the Jeep, which was engaged in four-wheel-drive, was constantly having to be dug free.

'Roy, looks like Hakawng Valley.'

On reaching the top of one of the ridges, Noel pointed eastwards towards rows of tightly packed hills, the Kumon mountains, and backbone of the Hakawng Valley. The extent of this mountainous terrain made it difficult to judge how far away we were from the Hakawng Valley, and as we pushed on into the mist our progress was further impeded by increasingly frequent and deeper river crossings. With the ever-increasing gradient we hit a particularly narrow section of track, blocked by a landslide. Congealed with samplings and undergrowth, this lump of earth took over an hour of 'landscaping' before we could drive on. Anxiously, we then inched the Jeep across a crumbling overhang - if it had given way, we would have fallen into the river below.

The cave-like atmosphere became more prevalent and the undulating terrain increasingly waterlogged as the day progressed. The terrain now fluctuated between hills, dried-up riverbeds scabbed with stones, and for much of the way, we used four-wheel-drive. At approximately 3,000 feet, it became increasingly cold, and with the onset of dusk, a veil of pearl-white mist spread over the tree canopy.

Three hours later, caked in mud, and desperate for food and shelter, we arrived at a small tribal settlement scattered with livestock and barefoot children. One of the residents spoke a little English and once we'd exchanged greetings, invited us into his hut. This was a small dwelling with an earth floor, bunches of herbs, animal skins, and a flyblown goat carcass hanging from the rafters.

Noel and I squatted on the earth floor drinking a sepia-coloured liquid with bark and leaves masquerading as tea, while trying to avoid the acrid smoke from the log fire. Our hosts confirmed we were still in the Hakawng Valley, but we were unable to define how far we were from Hell's Gate, or Ledo. These friendly people found accommodation for us in a bamboo shack smelling of goat urine. It made an ideal shelter, and after rustling up a meal we sat late into the night discussing our petrol crisis over the last of the whisky.

From the luminous dial on my watch, it had just gone 5.00 a.m. Shivering, I sat on the edge of my camp bed as the mist suspended in the air like wet smoke. With breakfast quickly over, we attended to the loose holding bracket on the alternator, which was causing the drive belt to slip, then enlisted the help of a couple of villagers to push-start the Jeep which had gone down with flat battery. Five hours later we were still driving through the dynamic Hakawng Valley. The probability of running out of fuel was now imminent: the fuel gauge was pegged at zero.

'That's it,Roy.' Noel pressed the starter but there was no response. In the faint hope the engine may have stalled through a blockage in the fuel

The Ledo Road.
Wild mules flee into the undergrowth.

pipe, I checked the main tank under the passenger seat: it was empty.

In advance of running out of petrol, we'd agreed I would walk to the Indian frontier, which would take about three days, then hopefully return with a full jerry can. Before setting off, we tried to define our exact location by climbing to the top of a rocky outcrop, from where we could see the frontiers of China, India, Tibet and Burma converge. Over in the northeast, at 19,296 feet, the snowy peak of Burma's Mount Hkakabo Razi, the highest mountain in Southeast Asia, was partially lost to the clouds. To the northwest were the shadowy passes of the Naga Hills, and beyond lay Assam, our nearest benchmark for India.

'See what you come up with, Roy. I reckon we're about 26 45' north, 96 10' east. Possibly closer to the Indian frontier than we thought.' Noel handed me the map and compass.

'We're about 45 miles from the border – a decent map would help.' I

gazed at the vast, brooding landscape with trepidation, knowing that I'd shortly be walking through this little-known region. Checking the contents of my survival rucksack which included Doc,[6] my rag-doll mascot, I clipped a full water bottle onto my belt, pocketed the map and compass, then synchronised watches with Noel.

'I'll have knocked off 10 miles before making camp for the night.' I slipped my parang into its scabbard.

'More like 15.' Noel joked, as we shook hands. *'By the way, don't forget to come back.'*

Before disappearing out of view, and dropping into a steady walking rhythm, I waved to Noel. A mile along the track, a family of monkeys screeched through the overhead branches, temporarily jangling my nerves: I'd always carried an automatic on jungle operations in Malaya, and felt vulnerable armed with just a parang. Several paces further on, I noticed a series of indentations in the earth, which looked like hoof- or footprints. While tracing these indefinite marks, the vegetation rustled, sending the survival instinct of my jungle days flooding back. This time however, I was unarmed, so when a group of men, in tattered combat uniform exploded from the undergrowth, I almost blanked out. They were armed with American carbines, light automatics and a Bren gun.

My aim now was to assure them I wasn't a threat. Having survived numerous Communist attacks in Malaya, it seemed ironic I should meet my fate taking the scenic route back home to England. Satisfied I was not carrying a gun, I was allowed to lower my arms. In broken English, and much to my relief, they confirmed they were soldiers from the Burmese Army Frontier Regiment. Their only means of transport through this rugged terrain was by mule.

'Allowed to enter Burma at own risk. English! You English?' The head of the group, Captain Tun, read the endorsement inside my passport.

'You were warned, so what you do here, walking through the jungle to India?' He shook his head in disbelief as I began to explain.

'Only the English....It would be far better if you and your friend returned to our jungle base camp for some food before carrying on to India, which is another 25 miles down the track.' The distance was considerably less than we'd calculated - a mere ramble over the hills, which meant I could be at the Indian frontier in under five hours. I headed back to fetch Noel.

While the evening meal was cooking, we were given a tour of the camp. There was a cluster of bamboo huts for the soldiers, a cookhouse, mule shelter, along with a shack housing a transceiver and radio equipment. The radio operator was busy on the Morse key, but more importantly, the generator had a petrol engine - we were in luck. In Fort Brooke, I'd been dependent on fuel to operate the generator for the wireless. Similarly, fuel was the lifeblood for Captain Tun and his platoon.

To compensate for being short on cash, we had to devise an alternative means of persuading Captain Tun to part with a few gallons of his precious liquid. He'd expressed an interest in my Rolex Oyster, purchased in 1952, but the watch was totally reliable, and I was reluctant to let it go.

The Rolex Oyster which caught the attention of Captain Tun.

Eventually, we agreed to exchange two gallons of fuel for several bars of soap and ten Player's cigarettes. With 25 miles to drive to the Indian frontier, we thanked our new-found friends, and continued through the Burmese jungle as fingers of lightning ricocheted overhead. The storm continued all the way to the Indian frontier post of Hell's Gate. A handful of huts in a restricted area, Hell's Gate isn't identified on many maps, and certainly wasn't on ours. The frontier barrier was simply an aperture between two rock crevices, blocked by a wooden door with a mesh grill. Soaked to the skin, we literally hammered on India's back door until an armed soldier, carrying a hurricane lamp, peered through the grill. Startled to see two Englishmen, he disappeared to fetch a squad of armed soldiers.

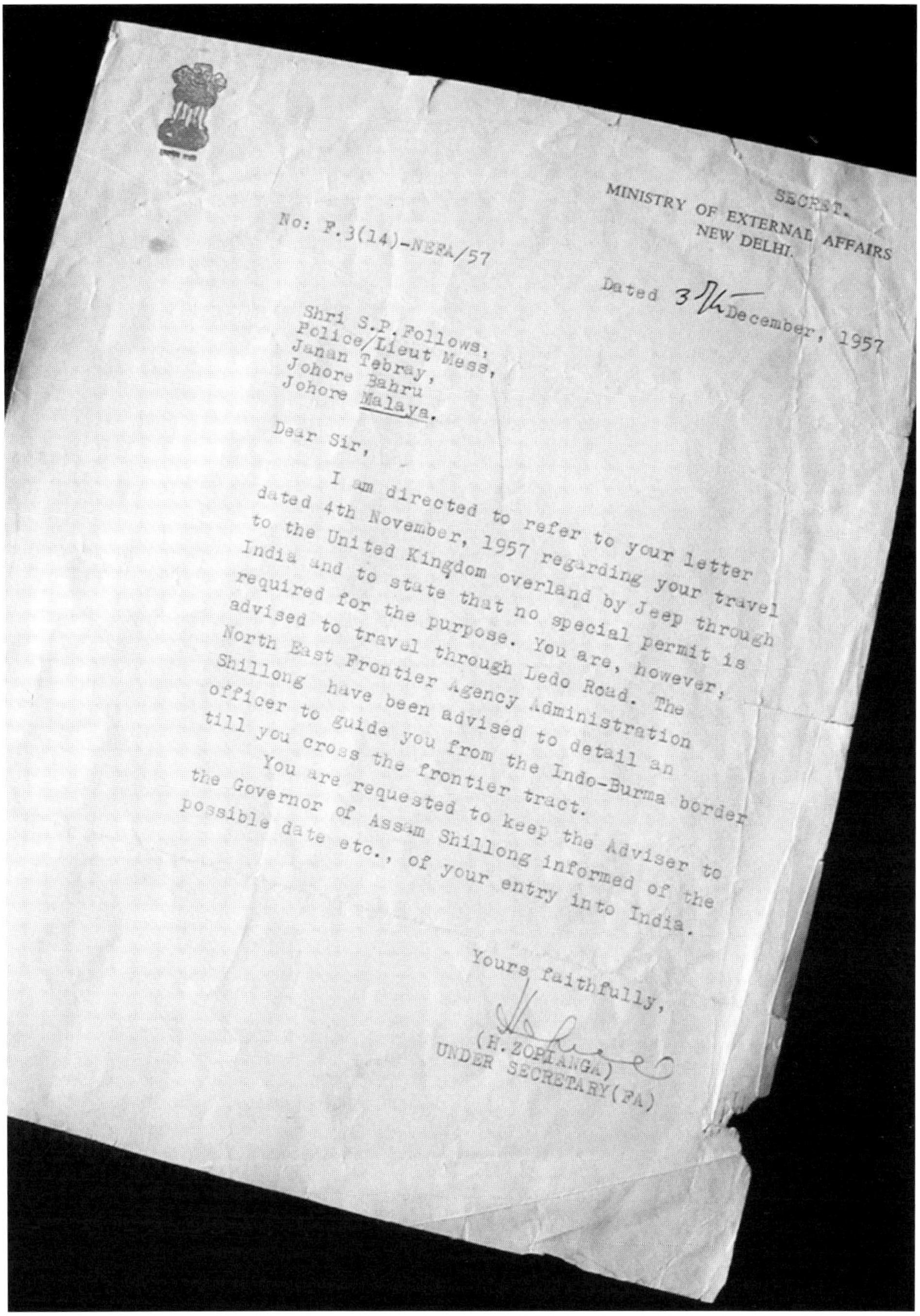
SECRET.

MINISTRY OF EXTERNAL AFFAIRS
NEW DELHI.

No: F.3(14)-NEFA/57

Dated 3rd December, 1957

Shri S.P.Follows,
Police/Lieut Mess,
Janan Tebray,
Johore Bahru
Johore Malaya.

Dear Sir,

I am directed to refer to your letter dated 4th November, 1957 regarding your travel to the United Kingdom overland by Jeep through India and to state that no special permit is required for the purpose. You are, however, advised to travel through Ledo Road. The North East Frontier Agency Administration Shillong have been advised to detail an officer to guide you from the Indo-Burma border till you cross the frontier tract.

You are requested to keep the Adviser to the Governor of Assam Shillong informed of the possible date etc., of your entry into India.

Yours faithfully,

(H.ZOPIANGA)
UNDER SECRETARY(FA)

'Secret' document issued by the Ministry of External Affairs, New Delhi.

Once we'd been thoroughly searched, the door was unbolted. Drenched and famished, we crossed the threshold, and slept on the border-post floor.

'Congratulations – all the way from Singapore.' The next morning, the officer in charge checked our paperwork. One of our documents, issued by The Indian Ministry of External Affairs, New Delhi, was classified *'secret'* and specifically for his attention. The document confirmed an officer from the North East Frontier Agency would 'guide' us from the 'Indo-Burma border' across the frontier tract to Ledo.

In addition to being experienced in jungle warfare, we were now adept at driving through dangerous terrain, so couldn't believe two military Jeeps were to escort us the last 15 miles to Ledo. Reluctantly sandwiched between the two vehicles, we departed Hell's Gate with a complimentary can of petrol from the officer in charge. An hour later we eased into Ledo, where the captain of the escort presented us with a bag of warm fruit and broken biscuits. It was a great relief to have successfully driven the complete length of the Ledo Road, which included some of the most challenging terrain in the world.

Endnotes

[1] In addition to filling the fuel tank,we purchased several cannisters of fuel: in total 40 gallons.

[2] We'd only met the head of Special Branch a couple of times, but this incident justified bending the truth, and sufficiently impressed the border guard.

[3] We had a spare spring – there were none available locally.

[4] 'Hakawng' is pronounced 'Hang'.

[5] Secondary jungle, is jungle that has been been cut back and the re-growth is significantly more dense. In contrast, primary or virgin jungle, has never been cut.

[6] See Appendix IV. Page 201. A note on Doc.

PLIEUT I

CHAPTER 5

DARJEELING DETOUR

Preparing to cross the Ganges with
a couple of sacred cows.

CHAPTER 5

DARJEELING DETOUR

From Ledo we continued unescorted to Digboi where we were hoping to exchange traveller's cheques. We never did find a bank, but the Jeep caught the attention of a couple of British expatriates working at a nearby oil complany. Recognising our plight, they invited us to their private club, rallied round the other club members enabling us to exchange some of our undeclared sterling into rupees.

With ready cash and good company, we spent an evening in the club bar, drank oceans of liquor and paid for the consequences the following morning. Fortunately, our hosts were also under par and were sympathetic, so we spent another day at the club to 'recover.'

The journey from Digboi to the temporary ferry mooring on the banks of the Brahmaputra at Goalpara took a couple of days. Notorious for its unpredictable flooding, from its source in Tibet, the Brahmaputra is fed by numerous tributaries as it makes its way through northeast India to join the Ganges. The caretaker of a nearby lodging house had warned us about the dangerous Brahmaputra, but this mighty river was only a mile wide at Goalpara, and therefore we crossed with relative ease.

40 miles from the disembarking point, the Jeep's engine started to smoke, omit a distinct smell of burning oil, followed by a drop in oil pressure. This time, the main oil pipe had fractured. To compound the problem, the pipe was flexible, and we didn't have a spare or relevant welding tools.

To find a mechanic, we needed to walk, or hitch to Cooch-Behar, the nearest town, and our next destination point. With the exception of a few ox-carts, the road ahead was desolate, but we managed to flag down a timber lorry, the first vehicle that passed by. Although we were unable to establish where the bemused Tibetan driver was going, he accepted some cigarettes, and took Noel aboard.

Four hours later, the sight of an approaching bus stuffed with passengers and poultry, sent the children from the nearby village, who'd tried to snaffle things off the Jeep scurrying home. When the vehicle rattled to a halt next to the Jeep, I could just pick out Noel trying to squeeze though the crowd.

'Worse than the No 53 from Manchester on a Saturday night.' Passing me a copper pipe, he jumped down. *'Specially made – not flexible.'*

Above & below: PLIEUT 1 crossing the Brahmaputra at Goalpara.

Noel's hitch had taken him to Cooch-Behar, where he'd been unable to buy a new oil pipe, but had managed to find a tinsmith to make one. Unfortunately, because the replacement copper pipe wasn't flexible, and was about an inch too long, it took a couple of hours to fit. With the pipe replaced, we headed for Cooch-Behar. Although the Jeep's headlights were still out of order, if there was sufficient moonlight, we intended to drive through the night to make up for lost time.

On approaching the frontier of Bhutan, the temperature dropped as the sun lit the white Himalayan peaks before slipping behind the horizon. Unprotected against the biting cold, we pushed on through remote villages where a yapping dog or flicker of light from a paraffin lamp, was the only sign of life.

Three hours later, we turned off the track, towards a wash of light which looked like a village. Approaching the glow, it soon became apparent that we'd driven into the grounds of a private tea planters' house. Two guards quickly blocked the drive, making it impossible to retreat.

'Dorothy Gibbs. May I help you?' A cut-crystal voice sliced through the night air, as an English lady, in full evening dress, opened the front door. We were all momentarily speechless.

Accepting our appologies, but unable to comprehend our plans to camp on the roadside, Mrs Gibbs insisted we took guest rooms in the house and joined the dinner party. Obliged to accept the invitation, we began the tedious job of unloading the Jeep to find our decent clothes, before joining Mr Gibbs, and guests, for pre-dinner drinks in our jungle greens. In sharp contrast to previous meals, dinner that evening was an elegant affair: attentive waiters flitted about the dining room serving fine food on fine china.

The next day, after breakfast with our hosts, we headed northwest towards Siliguri, where a signpost, with almost illegible lettering caught Noel's eye.

'D A R J E E L I N G'.

'Chance of a lifetime. What d' you say, Roy? It's only about 75 miles off course – could be worth the detour.'[1]

We tacked off in the direction of the sign, then as the altitude increased, changed into our thicker, ex-army tank suits to compensate for the drop in temperature. The road and railway up to Darjeeling looped about each other for most of the way and none of the 30 or more level crossings had gates or warnings. Kanchenjunga rose above the clouds while, to the north-west, a panoramic vista of the Himalayas stretched to infinity.

At an altitude of about 7,550 feet above sea level, Darjeeling[1] is famous for both its fine tea and narrow-gauge steam railway. During my late teens I'd helped to overhaul a number of steam leviathans including *The Coronation Scot* and *The Princess Margaret Rose.* Darjeeling's railway, one of the steepest and narrowest in the world, had always fascinated me. The quaint, pocket-sized engines which pulled miniature rolling stock were reminiscent of those toy trains found in amusement parks. Made in England at the turn of the 20th century, these 'toy trains' provided an invaluable service, snorting up and down the mountain transporting passengers and goods several times a day.

After ten years of independence, Darjeeling still retained much of its English character: The Windamere Hotel – a gem of a place, a red posting box, St Andrew's Church, and numerous streets with English names. We pulled up next to a colonial-style house with a sign. 'OC British Army Gurkhas.' planted in the front lawn. On the off chance of being able to sleep in the Gurkha depot - the Malay Police and Gurkhas have close ties, we knocked on the door.

'Its Noel. Dad, it's Noel, Noel Dudgeon.' June Amos, the daughter of Gurkha, Major Fred Amos, opened the door. Noel knew the Amos family from the time he was stationed with Fred in Malaya. We couldn't believe our luck.

Fred arranged for us to stay at the Gurkha officers' mess near to Tiger Hill, which is famous for its magnificent dawn view of Kanchenjunga. At first light the following day, where the sprawling bulk of Kanchenjunga pierced the clouds, plumes of snow streamed off its icy peak. Everest, a grey, icy wedge, towered above the jagged fangs of the Himalayas to our west. For the view alone, the detour to Darjeeling, the last Shangri-La, was worthwhile.

One afternoon, while studying our military maps of Sikkim and the Himalayas over a beer in the Windamere Hotel, an Indian character, introducing himself as 'Mathis,' sauntered over to our table and insisted on buying a round of drinks. Given his overt interest in the work we undertook in Malaya, we assumed he was a reporter for a local newspaper, after a story, but when he suggested we moved to a 'quiet corner' to look at our maps (which were recently charted, and not available to the general public), there seemed an alternative agenda.

'what's the proposition? If you're a journalist after a story we want cash up front, no State Bank of India cheque.' Mathis didn't appreciate our humour.

Above: The famous narrow-gauge railway leading up to Darjeeling. Noel looks on.
Below: A view of Darjeeling.

'Just say I'm an organiser, a fixer, and leave it at that, shall we?' Tossing a pack of Lucky Strike onto the table, he invited Noel to help himself.

'Listen.' An unlit cigarette balanced precariously on his lower lip. *'You are just the men I'm looking for. Used to long, challenging treks, able to navigate across difficult country, and to top it all, you have the maps of the area concerned. How would you like to earn some big money, some real cash?'*

'Big money. How much, and what's expected?'

'An American expedition team have lost all their film and camera equipment while crossing a river in Tibet. They were hoping to film the Yeti.'[2]

'The Yeti? An American blunder? Where do we come in?' Noel ordered another round of drinks.

'I need you to take replacement film equipment to them.' Mathis pulled on his cigarette. *'The expedition is sponsored by Coca-Cola, who want to film the Yeti for an advertising campaign. Believe me, this isn't a joke. We can offer big money.'*

Unfolding our maps, Mathis indicated the spot where, (according to the Sherpas who'd returned with the news of the lost equipment) the expedition was stranded.

'Look, this is Yeti country, not far over the Tibetan border from Nepal.'

Noel ran a finger over the map, going north-north-west from Darjeeling, crossing through part of Nepal into Tibet, and on to the spot Mathis had identified.

'About 100 miles, more with all the detours. Should be interesting, Roy. It's worth the risk for a hundred and ten pounds.' Although we had reservations about Mathis, we were so intrigued by the prospect of this detour we decided to take up his offer.

'By the way, you'll need visas for Nepal, but since you're English, it's just a matter of having your passport stamped by the Nepalese Consulate here in Darjeeling, and filling in a couple of forms.'

'How much film equipment is there?'

'No, no, don't worry about that. You will only need to carry your personal things in your rucksacks. Sherpas and pack mules will carry everything else.'

That afternoon, when we visited an expedition supplies agency with Mathis, he was greeted by a number of Sherpas, which implied he was well known. Although not involved with Mathis or the 'Coca- Cola' project, it was here we had the honour of speaking at length with Tenzing Norgay, the Nepalese mountaineer, who climbed Everest with Edmund Hillary in 1953.

Two days later, when we met up with Mathis to collect our visas. He was looking distinctly fraught and smoking nervously. *'I've some bad news. Take a seat.'* An empty pack of Lucky Strike lay on the table.

'Your visas, I don't understand. My friend at the Nepalese Consulate has been unable to process your visa applications here in Darjeeling, so the papers have now gone to the head of immigration in Kathmandu. I've never known this to happen. Processing your visas may now take at least two weeks, and its possible they may not be granted.' He drew on the butt of his cigarette. *'Perhaps it's because you're police officers – this job has different connotations in different countries.'*

There was no guarantee we'd be granted visas for Nepal. Additonally, waiting in Darjeeling for possibly two weeks would be a drain on our expenses, plus if we did go ahead with this venture, the consequent delay to our journey would result in being caught up in the Indian monsoons. With these thoughts in mind we called the venture off, and thereafter Mathis declined to reveal any further details. The following morning we collected the Jeep from the garage, called on the Amos family to say goodbye, then headed south for the Ganges.[3]

Down on the hot plains of West Bengal, we drove through the narrow corridor of Indian territory that lies between Nepal and Bangladesh. Somewhere along this route, as we tried to avoid a goatherd which shot in front of the Jeep, we hit a sacred cow. Noel slammed on the brakes but to no effect, and as metal hit hide, the poor beast, decorated with garlands and painted horns, crumpled to the floor. A mob of Hindus brandishing lengths of wood surrounded the Jeep. Two men then climbed on the back, while a couple of others grabbed at our clothes. While defending himself with one arm, Noel managed to pull away, scatter the mob, and gain sufficient speed to ensure the two men hanging on the back of the Jeep lost their grip and fell off.

This time, the brake failure was the result of a fractured brake pipe. Using our tried and tested method of chewing gum and a one-inch nail, we were able to blank-off the offending pipe. Continuing south through the parched landscape to Malda, we crossed a couple of rivers by barge, then made camp.

Top: The meeting with Tenzing Norgay made headlines in the Staffordshire 'Evening Sentinel.'
Above: A signed photograph of Tenzing Norgay, given to the author.

We were up before dawn the next day, and after a snack from a roadside stall, headed due south, arriving at a temporary ferry mooring on the Ganges. Desperate to shade from the afternoon sun, we pulled up next to the bleached skeleton of a solitary tree. Impervious to the flies and rotting detritus, several women were pounding washing against stones in the river, while their male counterparts attended dung fires, or wallowed with their cattle in the river.[4] The Ganges was about five miles wide at this point, and as we scanned through the haze that enveloped the opposite bank with our field glasses, we could just make out a smudge of buildings on the horizon.

In advance of the ferry arriving, the radiator was patched with a fast-drying plastic compound, refilled with the 'miracle' Ganges water, then in true local spirit, we washed a pile of clothes, and tossed them over the Jeep to dry.

The ferry was a frail-looking vessel with two pipes protruding from the hull: the exhaust emitting thick diesel fumes, and the bilge throwing up effluent. Part of the deck was roofed and served as temporary farmyard for a goatherd and several crates of chickens. Once the ferry was moored up, the skipper, an emaciated man with reed-like legs, dipped himself into the water, cupped his hands to take a drink, then picked his way across the silt, like a wading bird.

'Too hot. Sahib liking cross Ganga?' 'Wading Bird' inclined his head towards the opposite bank.

'Yes. When you go?'

'Go when cows come, no wait long, sahib.' Indifferent to the water dribbling down his legs he continued twisting his sodden dhoti.

The tinkling of bells marked the arrival of a herd of cows, which in spite of our three-hour wait, took priority for boarding. One by one, they were coaxed up two parallel ramps and onto the deck. Then it was our turn to join the Noah's Ark. Noel aligned the ramps to the width of the Jeep's wheels, then inched the Jeep forward. At the halfway point, the wheels started to skid on the cow dung. Once the tyres had regained their grip, the Jeep shot up the ramp, narrowly missed a couple of cows, then bolted across the deck where a gunwale stopped it from going over the side.

'A close one, Roy. Thought I was in the river.' Noel sat behind the steering wheel, while one of the crew and I pushed the Jeep into position so as not to upset the trim of the 'ferry.' The crew then pulled in the ramps, punted the vessel free from the silt until the engine kicked in, and

Waiting to cross the Ganges.

the floating farmyard drifted into the restless water. It was 5.00 p.m.

The ferry took the scenic route upstream to a village on the opposite bank. Tempted by a bloated ox carcass, flocks of vultures circled overhead, then as the sun began to slip below the horizon, the sky turned grey and the water changed from sepia to oily black. Progress was slow and steady, until we sailed through a raft of water hyacinths where the engine stopped. The methodical beat of water slapping against the hull cut through the silence.

'What's the problem?' Noel approached one of the crew.

'Engine no go, Sahib, mechanic man have much troubles.' He pushed his greasy cap to the back of his head.

Trapped by the current, broadside-on, the ferry's timbers began to groan, and as each wave slapped her side, she listed over until the current turned her 180 degrees and we headed back down the Ganges to our departure point.

'Water in fuel, sahib.' Squeezed between the engine and the bulkhead,

the mechanic frantically working the bilge pump, *'Main tank have plenty water, diesel pump have water, all fuel lines have water, heavy troubles, I no liking, Sahib.'*[5]

The ferry was now out of control, and with the fuel contaminating the water, it would be impossible to start the engine. Once the current took grip, we swirled down the river like a piece of driftwood, and the cows started to relieve themselves all over the deck. There was no lifesaving equipment on board, but in the event of needing to 'abandon ship' we did earmark a couple of rubber tyres that were being used as fenders.

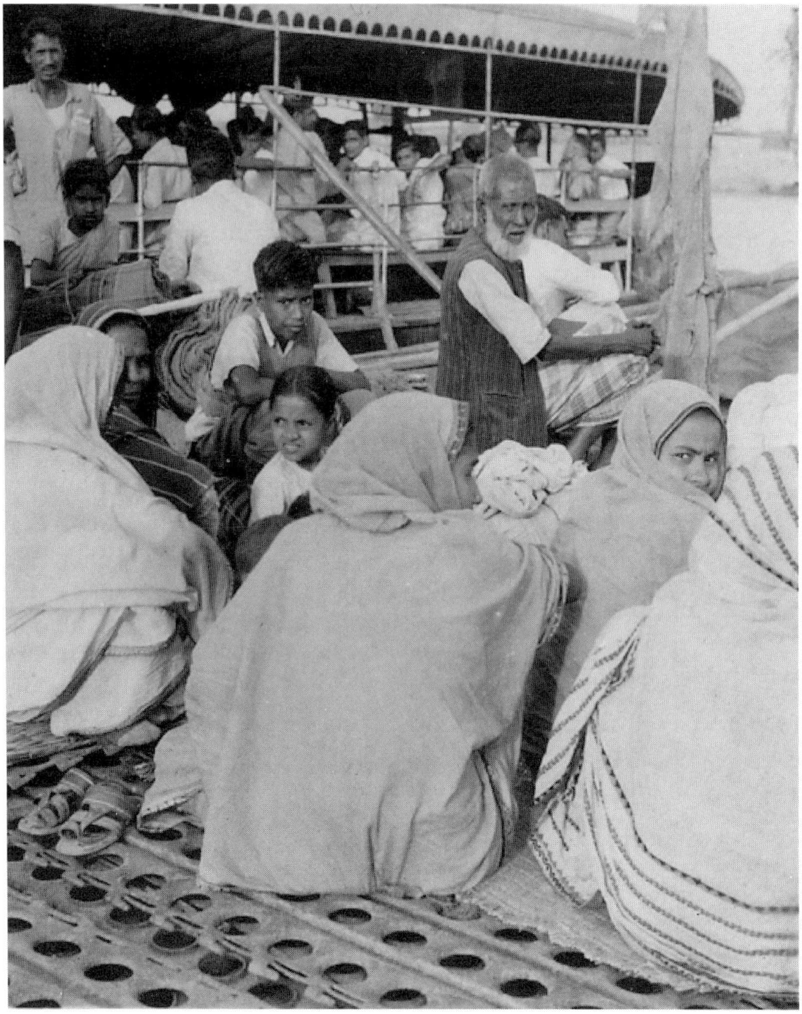

Travelling companions crossing the Ganges.

'The rate we're going, Roy, we could end up in Calcutta.' Looking through the darkness, we could just pick out freckles of light dotted along the riverbank. It was well over three hours since we'd cast off.

'Engine finished, sahib, we try stop riverbank later.' From 'Wading Bird's' explanation we understood the strong current was likely to subside the further we moved downstream. The helmsman planned to beach the craft at an appropriate point, before entering the busy part of the Ganges.

'In the dark?' I shook my head, looking at Noel. *'This should be good.'*

15 minutes later the ferry started to head towards the riverbank which was dense with trees and undergrowth. One of the crew sounded the depth with a bamboo pole, then shouted his findings to the helmsman in his little hut as we edged in. Once a suitable depth was established, the grappling iron, which had previously failed to hold the ferry upstream, was flung over the side. Although the anchor rope tightened as it took the strain, the ferry continued ploughing towards the shore. We braced ourselves for the impact, then as the grappling iron hit the riverbed, the bow peaked out of the water, scattering cattle across the deck.

The angle of the mooring,'somewhere north of Calcutta,' made it impossible to reach the riverbank without first wading through the water to realign the ramps.[6] There was no obvious track from the mooring, and the immediate area was dense with vegetation and sludge. Difficult to negotiate in the dark, we intended to camp, then tackle our way out in the daylight, but having already assembled his cattle, the herdsman was making to leave. It had just gone 10.00 p.m.

'Roy, he seems to know where he's heading.' Noel flashed the torch. *'It's still working - wish the bloody headlights did.'*

Guided by the sound of cowbells, we followed the meandering path of the cattle herd, until the water-logged terrain made it impossible to keep up. As we frantically dug the Jeep free, a loud bellow rented the night, then the melodic bells fell silent.

'The bastards have gone.' I cursed, climbing back into the driving seat.

We managed to drive across a couple of arable fields towards a cluster of weak lights in the middle distance.

'Roy, slow down, shacks and animal pens at two o'clock.' Noel pointed a few degrees off to the right. *'Must be a track around.'*

Visibility was now so poor, on approaching the dwellings from the rear, we accidentally drove into a yard and disturbed a pack of sleeping dogs. Quickly reversing, we took a chance left turn, continued driving for an hour, until we hit India's main artery, the Grand Trunk Road, stretching 1,600 miles between Calcutta and the North-West Frontier.

Relieved to have arrived at an identifiable location, we set up camp on the roadside. In the fog of my dream a door creaked loudly on its hinges, rolling over to face the road, it became apparent the noise was coming from the wheels of a bullock cart lumbering towards me. The driver was sleeping, with his head slumped forward.

From our camp on the side of the Grand Trunk Road, we headed towards Dumka, north to Bhagaipur on the Ganges, then west through the state of Bihar towards the River Son. In preparation to catch the daily flatcar across the Son, we slept next to the Jeep in the secure compound of a government-run guesthouse.

This being India, our departure across the Son was delayed. Re-joining the Grand Trunk Road, we continued west for the holy, Hindu City of Varanasi where the temperature gauge shot into the red. This time, steam issued out of the top hose which we patched with a roll of adhesive plaster from the first-aid kit.[7]

Arriving in Varanasi later that afternoon, we nudged our way through crowds of pilgrims and tried not to inhale the smoke from the funeral pyres which choked the air. This was India in the raw.

Endnotes

[1] Darjeeling is a corruption of two Hindi words 'Dorje-Ling', which means 'Place of the thunderbolt.' Collins English Dictionary 1994.

[2] 'Yeti' is a translation of the Tibetan *metohkangmi*, from *metoh* foul, plus *kangmi*, meaning 'snowman'. Also called the abominable snowman, the yeti is a large, ape-like creature alleged to inhabit the Himalayas. Collins English Dictionary 1994.

[3] Several months after our Yeti opportunity, the Tibetans rebelled against the occupying Chinese military. This ill-fated uprising was spearheaded by CIA-trained Tibetans operating in the area where the American 'expedition' team were hoping to film the Yeti. The expedition may have possibly been a cover-up for something more politically complex.

[4] Sacred to the Hindus, the Ganges is reputed to be the largest open sewer in the world. Animal and human corpses, along with ashes from the deceased, plus thousands of tons of human effluent are discharged into the river every day. The Ganges is also a major source of domestic water from which the Hindus bathe and drink with impunity.

[5] The engine (a former six-cylinder diesel tractor-power unit fitted with a reduction gear linked to the propeller shaft) was in a dungeon-like hole with several inches of oily water sloshing about.

[6] To date, we've been unable to locate exactly where this ferry beached along the Ganges.

7 The spare hose had already been used, and we'd been unable to buy a replacement.

SINGAPORE GREAT BRITAIN
OVERLAND
FM
JA 6178

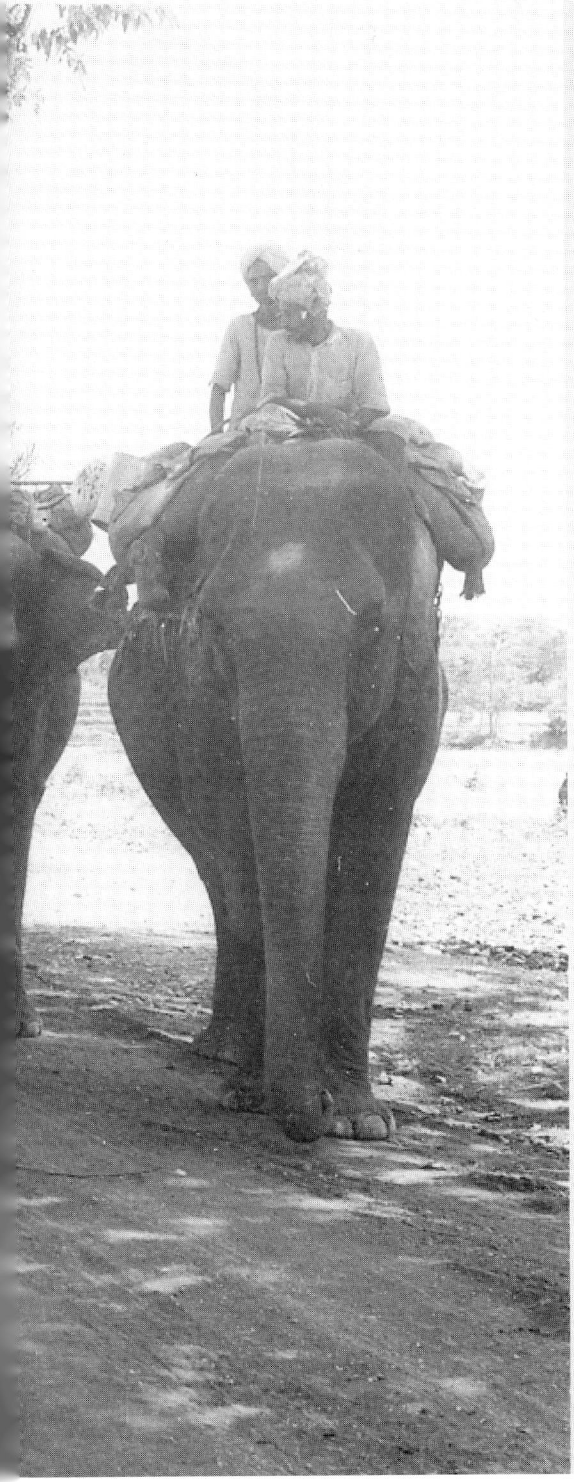

CHAPTER 6

AMBUSH

The Grand Trunk Road approaching Delhi.

CHAPTER 6

AMBUSH

Allahabad was simmering with festival activity. Snake-charmers, acrobatic monkeys, professional letter-writers, stalls selling used false teeth, and magicians swallowing live chickens all had their place.[1] As we edged through the streets looking for a bank, we were initiated into the festival spirit with a shower of carmine-coloured powder, saturating our hair and clothes.

'Fancy seeing him outside your local.'

In a vain attempt to remove the coloured dust from his clothes, Noel inclined his head towards a fakir with waist-length, matted hair. Covered in grey ash, and almost naked, as he clasped his hands in prayer, no one else gave him a second glance.

The bank offered no refuge from the festival chaos: everyone was frantically waving their arms, desperate to be served. A punkah wallah squatting in a corner, pulled the cord of his reed punkah with such complacency, it hardly moved the stifling air. Having missed our turn several times, we forced our way to the counter, and thereafter were shunted from clerk to clerk, before finally being ushered into a dusty office and introduced to the chief cashier.

The 'Chief' was reluctant to exchange ten pounds of traveller's cheques into rupees and, since the bank was now due to close, suggested we made an 'out of hours' appointment with the bank manager. Desperate for cash, we waited outside as instructed. Once the main doors of the bank were locked, a Sikh armed guard led us through a side entrance into the bank manager's office. Two portraits – Nehru, the Indian Prime Minister, and Ganesa, the Hindu god of prophecy, looked down from the wall at the papers littering his desk.

'Take a seat, take a seat.'

The bank manager swatted a wad of documents from a couple of chairs then ordered the guard to bring tea. We sat anxiously for a couple of minutes while he leafed through our papers, then, much to our relief, he authorised the transaction; It had taken over three hours to exchange just ten pounds of traveller's cheques into rupees.

Leaving Allahabad, we passed through Kanpur, and made camp among a coppice of roadside trees.[2] Although we'd lost quite a bit of time in

Allahabad, we clocked up 324 miles that day, the best run since leaving Singapore six weeks previously. we were, however, concerned about one of the front wheel bearings. It had been rattling like a bag of nails for the last 35 miles, and since we didn't have spares or appropriate tools to fix it, we were reliant on it holding out for the 275 miles to Delhi.

The following morning, the ground was covered in a tulle-like mist and the sun barely over the horizon. We broke camp without making a brew to ensure we'd reach Delhi before nightfall, but were unable to gun the starter until the spark plugs had been heated over the flames of the cooking stove.

Cows, elephants, buses and bullock carts were all vying for space along the Grand Trunk Road approaching Delhi. Entering the city we passed several notable landmarks: the Red Fort with its massive sandstone wall, the Secretariat block, parliament building, and finally India Gate, the towering stone arch dedicated to the 85,000 Indian soldiers.[3]

With the repairs to the Jeep taking several days, we booked into a cheerful, inexpensive hotel, dropped the Jeep off at a nearby garage, then had our first haircut since leaving Singapore. Before we'd committed to sitting down, the barber had plucked a razor from a nearby shelf and flung a grey shroud across my shoulders.

'Sahib, I am Aziz. Sit, sit, I shave all off, just like Yul Brinner?' Reluctantly I eased into the chair.

'Ah Sahib, The King and I *very good film. Very good haircut. Aziz* spat on the blade. *Sahib keep moustache?'* A sickly smell of patchouli and warm jasmine filtered through the air.

'No moustache, no beard – all off please.' The razor blade sliced through the air and landed on my Adam's apple with butterfly delicacy. Each time Aziz coughed, sniffed, or was momentarily distracted by the backing music from the radio, an edge of cold steel skated across my face – it was impossible to relax.

'Sahib much earwax.' Aziz pushed my head over to inspect then took a bamboo sliver from a nearby jar. *'Let me clean out, please, I have diploma from Calcutta, where I learn business. Won't hurt Sahib.'*

'No. Don't touch ears. Haircut and shave only.' Calcutta diploma or not, I didn't relish the thought of my ears being poked with a bamboo skewer, particularly since it had been used on a previous client.

'Sahib try massage?' His dextrous fingers started to pummel the back of my neck.

'Sahib feel better?' 'Sahib' was now exhausted, but the kneading continued, then just when I thought my ordeal was over, the lather boy smothered a scalding, jasmine-scented towel over my face.

'More aromatic oil, Sahib?' My muffled protests went unheard.

'Ah! This is Himalayan Poppy, Sahib smell pretty.' Slipping his eyes over to Noel who was undergoing similar treatment, Aziz applied another dollop of lotion to my stinging face. We'd only called in for a quick haircut and shave, but ended up having the works and smelling like a pair of gigolos.

Suitably cleaned up, after advising the Foreign Office of our safe passage through Burma, we visisted the Yugoslav and Iranian embassies with a view to acquiring visas. During the late 1950s, Yugoslavia actively discouraged foreign visitors, and in line with the policies of the day, our application was declined. We'd anticipated this reaction, but politely agreed to re-apply at the Yugoslav embassy in Istanbul. In contrast, the Iranian embassy issued visas without ceremony, along with advice about potentially dangerous sand-drifts.

We'd covered over 1,000 miles with defective brakes and headlamps which the mechanic had now repaired, but he seemed desperately flustered.

'*Flippy-floppy not working. Don't have spare, can't fix. Wheels, springs, brakes, clutch, all things I make good, but this flippy-floppy I can't do.'* Reaching inside the Jeep, he pointed towards the disfunctional windscreen assembly, which was the least of our worries.

With the fuel and food supplies topped up, it was time to move on to Amritsar, the Punjab capital, and nucleus of the Sikh religion. Free from the time restraints and formalities of hotel living, we left Dehli feeling confident. The wind snatched at the canvas hood as we bumped along at almost 50mph, then without warning the oil pressure dropped.

The oil had been topped up when the engine was overhauled in Delhi, but the dipstick was now registering empty. There was also a distinct smell of 'fry-up,' but the crankcase and engine seemed free of leaks. On removing the oil-filter cap, a wisp of blue smoke curled up from the intake: a clear indication that the engine was burning up the oil. The spare pint of oil wasn't enough because the sump alone held about a gallon and a quarter.

Our only option was to return to the previous village we'd driven through, which was seven miles away, and try to buy oil.

It was my turn to walk or hitch this time. Grabbing a few dry chapattis to stave off my hunger, I started to walk along the traffic-free road. After a couple of minutes I flagged down a lorry with a bunch of plastic flowers hanging from the radiator grill. Two Sikhs in saffron-coloured robes emerged from the cab. They'd passed Noel, and realising we were not a threat, offered to give me a hitch. I clambered aboard and made myself comfortable between a couple of rice sacks.

Ten minutes later we pulled up outside a dilapidated building and crude notice-board advertising 'Motor Products,' where I was able to buy a gallon can of oil, before thanking the Sikhs, as we continued our separate ways.

During the heat of the day, most drivers take a nap, and the chance of hitching back to Noel seemed unlikely. I established a steady pace while taking frequent drinks from my water bottle, but knew that my shaven head and ragged clothes looked unsavoury, and therefore the few vehicles that passed by ignored my plea for a hitch. It was impossible to keep a steady pass while constantly having to swap the oil canister from one hand to another, but after about three miles, a bell-like noise sounded some way behind me. Looking through the mirage of heat, I could just pick out a cyclist meandering down the centre of the road in a ghostly-looking dhoti. He fell to a halt, and addressed me in his native tongue, filling the air with the stench of stale liquor.

Although he didn't speak English, and I certainly had no command of Hindi, his battered features collapsed into a drunken smile when I mentioned the word 'backsheesh.' Straddling the rusty carrier over the rear wheel, and with the oil canister balanced between my legs, we wobbled off down the centre of the road, then at each incline, I dismounted, while he pushed the cycle.

On reaching Noel, the old cyclist received his well-deserved backsheesh then tacked-off down the centre of the road. With the oil replenished, we headed cautiously to Amritsar, spending the night alongside the Jeep in the garage of a government rest house to ensure our belongings would be safe.

The city of Amritsar, in the northwest Punjab, is the centre of the Sikh religion and is 20 miles from the Indian frontier with Pakistan. At this point India and Pakistan is divided by just 50 yards of no man's land, so we had to negotiate two lots of red tape within a very short distance.

Firstly, at the Indian frontier, two armed police poked about the Jeep, checking the chassis and engine numbers corresponded with the carnet. Meanwhile, we were ordered into an office for the familiar procedure of form filling,questions and baksheesh. Determind not to hand over any money, it took over an hour before the barrier was lifted. 50 yards on, the process was repeated at the Pakistan frontier. Again, we didn't concede, but in total, 'bribe time' wasted over three hours.

The stench of Lahore, where it was hot enough to fry an egg on the engine cover, slapped us around the face like the scalding-hot towels used by the barber in Delhi. Although only 16 miles from the Indian frontier, Lahore is the cultural centre of Pakistan, and in pre-partition days, its tree-lined streets gave it the appropriate name of the 'Paris of India'.

'Bribe time' at the Pakistan frontier.

From Lahore we were keen to drive on to Multan. The Jeep had been misfiring and consuming oil at an alarming rate. In the hope of nursing the engine, we changed the oil filter and heavily carbonised spark plugs - a sign that the valves needed to be replaced. Our efforts didn't improve the Jeep's performance, but we pushed on, stopping only to change drivers or top up the oil. On arriving in Multan late that evening, the market was still trading: gas lamps twinkled like jewels from every stall, and the smell of spice and jasmine filled the night air. Having only eaten a banana and a hand-full of stale chapattis all day, we wolfed down a plate of roast chicken at the first available food-stall.

Pressing on, we crossed the railroad bridge spanning the River Chenab, and just after midnight arrived in Muzaffargarh, where the Jeep's headlights disturbed a number of villagers sleeping on charpoys outside closed shops. That night we set up camp just off the road, on the outskirts of Muzzaffargarh. Dog-tired, we could barely muster a brew or bite to eat, and fell asleep in the clothes we'd worn since leaving Delhi.

Repairing a broken leaf spring, and more importantly, a fractured chassis, which opened and closed when the Jeep was bounced on its lifting handles, preoccupied our thoughts the following day. The terrain ahead,

Lahore.
London is 6,372 miles away.

which included the mountains of Baluchistan, was guaranteed to split the chassis. Completing the journey now hinged on finding a garage to undertake these essential repairs. How we wished we'd stayed in Lahore.

We spread our maps on the ground, trapping them against the wind with stones. Pakistan, Baluchistan and Iran were all illustrated, along with archaeological sites, and the routes taken by the invading army of Alexander the Great in the defeat of King Darius III. This historic information was all very interesting, but quite useless to anyone urgently needing a garage. The city of Quetta, formerly occupied by Alexander the Great, and 300 miles away, seemed our best option: we broke camp and headed due west.

Before long, we arrived at a narrow, makeshift bridge spanning the Indus, the largest river in Pakistan.[4] It was supported by a number of pontoons, and adjacent to its approach was a solitary tree bearing a hand-painted sign written in Urdu, which we were unable to translate.

Lifting our right hands we called out '*Saalam alay kum,*' the few words of Urdu we knew,[5] then drove onto the bridge as an exodus of camels, donkeys and people surged in our direction. Laden with bales of cotton, the camels creaked by with a slow, majestic gait, releasing a malodorous breath as they dipped their heads inside the Jeep. The women meanwhile recoiled behind yashmaks and the Pathan-looking men returned our greetings with obvious verbal abuse. Several days later we learned the sign advised the direction of the bridge-crossing changed on alternate days.

On reaching the far side of the bridge, we were flagged down by a young man. Speaking good English, he introduced himself as 'Abdullah', and asked if we'd take him to his home town of Dera Ghazi Khan (DGK), 25 miles away. We were initially reluctant to take Abdullah board, as any extra weight would aggravate the chassis, however when we heard that his brother was the manager of a transport company in DGK, and could possibly repair both the chassis and spring, we made room for him in the front of the Jeep, and sped off in a cloud of dust before he could change his mind.

DGK was a one-donkey town with single-storey mud buildings and a few dismal shops selling warm fruit drinks, condensed milk and fly-blown goat meat. We pulled up outside a wooden archway with a notice-board advertising the 'Punjab Transport Company'. This was only a sub-depot operating a fleet of vehicles between Karachi in the south and Rawalpindi and other cities in the north. The workshop and adjacent yard was full of welding equipment, including a vulcaniser for repairing punctures, and boxes of spares for the company's particular fleet of vehicles.

Camel Trouble.
One-way traffic crossing the Indus.

Abdullah's brother, Hamid, agreed to take on all the repairs and test the engine. To access the chassis, the Jeep was unloaded, manhandled over to 45 degrees, then propped up with timber. In the event of petrol leaking from the tank, Noel and I stood on hand with the fire extinguisher, watching sparks fly while the mechanic welded the metal plate over the fracture.

The engine valves and seatings, which having burnt out, caused excess oil consumption and power loss, proved too complex to repair, but for all his efforts, Hamid would only accept payment for a can of oil.

'Watch out for the Pathans.' Hamid gestured his right forefinger across his throat. *'For most of the way you'll be in the lawless tribal area of Baluchistan. That's why we don't operate that way. Good luck.'*

We departed DGK with the sharply-etched mountains dominating the horizon in a line of broken fangs. It was a merciless-looking landscape,and

Chassis repairs courtesy of the Punjab Transport Company.

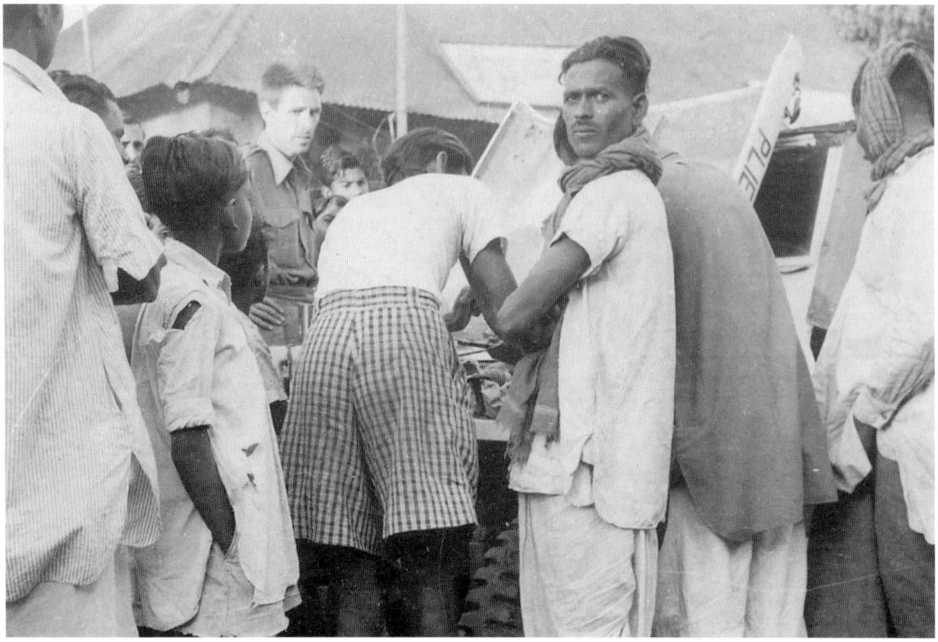

Repairs completed.
A final photo call with the Punjab Transport Company.

as the Jeep was still misfiring, the chance of reaching Quetta looked slim.

30 miles from DGK the stony track plunged into a rock-strewn ravine. Once we'd climbed the far side, we continued in low gear, stopping only to check the oil or clear fallen rocks from the track. By mid-afternoon we reached the hamlet of Mekhtar, with just a few stone huts surrounded by a group of belligerent-looking men armed with rifles. From Mekhtar the Jeep struggled through the craggy landscape of the Sulaimân Mountains

for another two hours until we reached Loralia. Now only 120 miles away, Quetta was in our grasp.

The stalls sprinkled along the pot-holed road leading into Loralia sold everything from intricate hammered brass, tooled leather, and Persian carpets to Afghan hashish, plastic combs, and firearms. With the exception of the plastic trash, nothing had changed during the last hundred years.

Adjacent to the stalls we found a makeshift tarpaulin hut masquerading as a restaurant where a group of armed Pathans were eating goat stew and spitting pieces of gristle onto the earth floor. Feeling distinctly uneasy, we quickly drank a bowl of goat stew, (there were no utensils), then headed up into the hills just outside Loralia, to find a safe spot to camp.

There were two routes from Loralia to Quetta. Given the state of the engine, plus the fuel shortage, we risked taking the shorter, albeit more dangerous route which was habited by the Pathan Rebels. Flocks of buzzards squabbling on rocky outcrops pierced the silence of the barren landscape. Then suddenly, as we stopped to remove boulders from the track, a series of screams shattered the air and a group of armed men leapt from behind a rock onto the track. They were all wearing bandannas long, taupe woollen coats, and brandishing rifles.

'Who are these bastards?'

We pressed our backs against the Jeep, and as they closed in, noticed some were also armed with knives. Whatever they planned to do – kill us, take our belongings, or simply chop our bollocks off for a laugh – we were at their mercy.

'Allah Akabar.' [6] Offering our best Arabic blessing, we didn't raise our hands or cower. Suitably thrown by our reaction, their aggression softened and the ugly situation fell flat like a failed schoolboy prank. Easily encouraged with cigarrettes, we soon established a rapport, and were even allowed to handle their .303 Lee-Enfield rifles, which had possibly been stolen from the British during the Colonial days. Confident they didn't view us as a threat, we assumed we would soon be allowed to drive on, but when the rifles were snapped back into place, and we were ordered into the Jeep, it seemed prudent not to argue. Like an adventure story out of *Boys' Own*, we were escorted to their mountain hideout where a rifleman standing by a stone lookout guarded the fortified approach.

The leader of the group indicated we'd be released the following day, and allowed us to roam within the boundaries of the camp. During the short time in captivity,(technically we were guests, albeit reluctant ones), we

Loralia to Quetta.
'We risked taking the shorter, more dangerous route.'

constantly maintained a positive rapport with our captors. This included giving a handful of tablets, which unknown to our captors would only cure a headache, to one of the elders with a fever. Sketching maps of our route in the sand, and making endless mugs of tea on the petrol cooking stove, which the Pathans had never previously seen, also helped to maintain a congenial atmosphere.

With the onset of dusk, we'd made considerable progress in gaining their trust, and joined our hosts around an open fire where they smoked and played cards. We slept in a wide rock cleft that evening, parking the Jeep in front of the aperture to deflect the bitter wind. The Pathans simply rolled into their animal skins then bedded down close to the fire, which glowed until dawn.

One of the men, a wiry, teak-faced character named Rasoul, threw his goatskin bag and sleeping roll into the back of the Jeep, then with the butt of his rifle nudging me in the ribs, squeezed between Noel and I. Although his extra weight would aggravate the engine, we were so relieved to be released we didn't question why he'd joined us, and departed to a cheering crowd.

Nervously tapping the butt of his rifle, Rasoul scanned the cliffs as we drove back to the point where we'd been ambushed. 12 miles into the journey he began to hammer his fist on the dashboard, indicating to stop. Stepping from the the Jeep, he cupped his hands to his mouth, and let out a booming call that reverberated through the mountains. A pair of buzzards floated down from their stony ledge to investigate, then a lone figure appeared from a vantage point brandishing a rifle. After a further exchange of calls, Rasoul returned to the Jeep. Ten minutes later, as we entered a ravine, the process was repeated. This time there was no reply. Gesturing for us to wait, he scrambled through the rocks with the rifle across his back until he was out of view.

Driving away without him was never an option. In his absence, we topped up the engine with oil and water. The sun grilled the ravine with impunity, and as the heat broiled off the rocks it created a natural kiln. An hour passed by before we were alerted by a distant call as Rasoul ran towards us, carrying an additional rifle. With sweat streaming down his face, he propped both rifles up against the Jeep, and when we offered him our water bottle, he guzzled the lot. Instead of guarding the outpost, we established that Rasoul had found his friend asleep, and had quietly removed his rifle for a prank.

On leaving the ravine where the boulder-studded landscape appeared almost lunar, Rasoul gave a final call into the mountains, shook our hands, then with both rifles, leapt across the rocks like a gazelle. This time, when two men joined him at the summit of the aguille, he held his rifle aloft indicating for us to leave. We were free.

Above: Preparing to leave the Pathan camp.
Below: Rasoul and Noel with the additional rifle.

Endnotes

[1] Due to the high rate of illiteracy, letter writing is considered a profession in India.

[2] Former name 'Cawnpore.' An industrial city in north-east India, on the River Ganges.

[3] During the Indian Mutiny of 1857, a small British Army Garrison was captured. Most of the soldiers and families were massacred by Nanah Sahib. Over one hundred British women and children were slaughtered. Their bodies are believed to have been disposed in a well.

[4] The Indus rises in southwest Tibet in the Kailas Range of the Himalayas, flows northwest through Kashmir, then southwest across Pakistan to the Arabian Sea. Length: 1,800 miles (2,900 km).

[5] *'Peace be with you.'*

[6] *'God is Great.'*

SINGAPORE GREAT BRITAIN
OVERLAND
FM
JA 6178

CHAPTER 7

SANDSTORM

The AKROPOLIS garage in Zahedan.
Dimitri is in the foreground.

CHAPTER 7

SANDSTORM

Relieved of our Pathan friends, we continued west through the mountains to Quetta where we stayed the night in the Chiltern Hotel. It felt marvellous to wash and change out of the same clothes we'd worn since Delhi.

There wasn't a garage in Quetta that would take on the responsibility of overhauling the Jeep, but the hotel manager introduced us to a Pakistani army major, in charge of the local army workshop, who agreed to overhaul the Jeep, on the proviso we'd have to wait for three days. On day three, the major pulled out, leaving us with no choice but to overhaul the failing engine ourselves.

With the old engine oil replaced with new, a cleaned crankcase, new set of plugs, points, and changed oil filter, we were ready to take on the 400-mile desert trail to the Iranian frontier. To ensure there'd be drinking water in the event of a breakdown, and the cooling system could be easily replenished, we'd filled up with water, plus an additional 30 gallons of fuel to hopefully compensate for the lack of outlets along the route.

We departed apprehensively from Quetta early the next day, and within a couple of miles, ascended a steep, dirt track between hills of igneous rock. Other than intermittent tyremarks, there was no evidence this was the main route to the Iranian frontier.

With the compass needle pointing west, we emerged on to the expansive desert plains, and pulled up at Sheik Wasil where the temperature hovered around 100 degrees farenheit as we filled up with oil and water. The unforgiving terrain from Sheik Wasil tested the springs to their limit, and made it almost impossible to talk.

'Noel, what the hell's that?' We pitched out of our seats as I stamped on the brakes.

'Wheel's off!' Noel motioned over to the right. The spare wheel, which had peeled away the holding bracket from the bodywork like the lid of a sardine tin, bounced across the desert.

Since the back of the Jeep was already overloaded, once retrieved, the spare was lashed onto the engine cover, which meant it had to be removed when topping up with oil or checking the engine. The jagged edges of the bodywork were the least of our worries, and simply flattened with the hammer.

Five hours later we reached Nok kundi, Pakistan's official, albeit desolate, frontier post, in the heart of a stony wilderness.[1] The usual fleet of guards failed to appear when we pulled up at the barrier, and apart from the sounds of the hot, swirling wind and creaking window shutters, the area was silent. Tentatively, we entered the sand-swept building, and to our relief, found a handful of immigration officials in various stages of sleep.

'Papers! Papers!' Dismissing our apologies for disturbing their siesta, one of the guards reluctantly stretched into action.

Nok Kundi.
Pakistan's official frontier post.

Mustn't ruffle this arrogant bastard, I thought, as he grabbed our document file, fired the usual stock-in-trade questions, then arrogantly prompted Noel for an *'Engleesh'* cigarette, before inclining his head towards the door, indicating for us to leave.

Heading towards the Iranian frontier, the engine started to lose compression, which made it difficult to maintain a speed above 25 miles per hour. The Jeep finally gave up in a real camel's areshole of a village: the fly-blown, desert oasis of Taftân. Much to our relief, the engine hadn't quite packed in, but the petrol pump was blocked with sediment. After fitting the spare pump, (we were unable to dismantle and clean the existing pump in this sand-swept, fly-infested environment), the Jeep burst into life. [2]

A few strands of rusty barbed-wire and a line picked out in the sand defined the frontier boundary, the wadi of no man's land which separated Pakistan from Iran. The Jeep was now losing compression, and as the wheels churned in sand, a group of Iranian border guards came to our rescue, and pushed us into Iran as the distinct smell of burning oil filled the air.

Having clocked up 400 miles in 13 hours, we were desperate to make camp, but one of the guards insisted on taking us to an 'official' checkpoint a few miles away, then on to Zahedan police station.

The additional 50 miles to Zahedan proved to much for the Jeep which packed in just outside the station compound. Despite the failing engine, we'd exceeded all our expectations, crossed some of the roughest terrain in the world, and covered a total of 1,900 miles in just ten days. The effects of the desert: sand-saturated clothes, cracked lips and sore eyes were now all too apparent. Relieved to be showered with tea and biscuits, we recovered in Zahedan police station while our documents were checked.

The Iranian police offered accommodation in a nearby lodging house. Formerly owned by a Sultan or Pasha, this opulent building was now almost derelict. A poor, Iranian family, consisting of an elderly prophet Hassan, along with his son Razak, who had a number of wives and children in tow, scraped together a meagre living from renting out a couple of the rooms.

Under the instruction of 'number-one wife' who dispensed orders from behind the veil of a black burka, we followed Razak up several flights of stairs to an attic room. A shaft of light from a narrow aperture in the thick stone walls ensured that even during the day, the room remained dark. It was also an ideal breeding ground for cockroaches, which rattled across the floor when disturbed by Razak's hurricane lamp.

Over the years, Noel and I had eaten all types of food in many strange and unhygienic circumstances, so we had no hang-ups in joining our Iranian hosts for supper. Beckoning us to sit, 'number-one wife' ladled a spicy meat concoction onto our plates. Suspecting the meat was rancid, but not wanting to offend our hosts, I turned to Noel who confirmed my reservations, tentatively raised a fork full of meat to my mouth, then swallowed hard while trying not to gag. It was impossilbe to continue eating, and the counter effect of suppressing nausea made me sweat. Feigning to have had a substantial meal earlier in the day, we excused ourselves from the table, then once out of sight I forced myself to vomit.

The Jeep had now been towed by the Iranian police to a local garage. This white-washed building, with the name 'AKROPOLIS' emblazoned in red letters across the wall, along with an Arabic transcript, showed no resemblance to the Athenian citadel of its namesake, but on meeting Dimitri the Greek owner, things fell into place.

Dimitri agreed to take on the Jeep repairs but, since we were unable to exchange traveller's cheques at the local bank, we had to devise an alternative means of payment. Similar to Captain Tun in Burma, Dimitri was keen to trade my Rolex, but I declined.

Once we'd driven through Iran, we were on the homeward run; the road conditions would improve, and the availability of garages and spare parts would be more prolific. This meant that many of the spare parts and equipment, including the winch tied to the front bumper, would be surplus to requirements. Dimitri agreed to take the winch in exchange for repairs and labour, on condition we demonstrated it was working. Apprehensively, we lashed it to an overhead beam in the workshop, secured a weight to the lifting hook, then cranked up the handle. Unaware there was sand in the mechanism, which prevented it from slipping, the winch passed Dimitri's test with flying colours.

Routing through a a pile of disgarded paint tins at the back of Dimitri's workshop we discovered a box containing the exact spares needed for the Jeep: an extraordinary find in the middle of Zahedan. Labelled 'US ARMY,' the box contained new valves, corresponding springs and a set of piston rings wrapped in greaseproof paper with the lettering 'WILLYS TOLEDO.'

During the three days we worked with Dimitri, the Jeep's engine was dismantled, the new valves ground into the cylinder head, and new piston rings fitted. Each evening, after a full days labour, we returned to the 'Pasha's Palace' and washed from a large cooking pot in the yard. The cold water from the outside well - the only water source available, didn't remove the black carbon grease, then to add insult to injury, we always managed to impregnate the soap with sand, and soak the clean, dry clothes we'd put to one side.

Repairs in progress.
The AKROPOLIS.

On the morning of our departure, Hassan asked us to translate a letter which he produced from the folds of his gown. It was written by an Australian travel agency on behalf of a group of friends proposing to take a holiday in Iran. Their itinerary included a visit to Zahedan, where they wanted to spend three nights in '*First class accommodation, with drinks bar, good food, air conditioning and extensive views.*'

While not wishing to insult Hassan, we explained that his Pasha's Palace wasn't up to the standard requested in the letter. Both Assan, and his son, who had a relatively good command of English, failed to see why. Keen to seize the opportunity of making some money, Hassan asked if we'd reply to the letter, outlining the cost and facilities of the accommodation. In the knowledge that we'd be well out of town before the Australian guests set foot on Iranian soil, we penned a fine reply detailing the *'superior facilities, luxurious bathrooms, and extensive views.'* Offering profuse thanks, Hassan signed, and slipped the letter into its return envelope. Minutes later, we were heading for Bam.

Chiefly consisting of a high, central desert plateau, Iran is about six times the size of the British Isles. Almost completely surrounded by mountains, Iran stretches 1,700 miles from the Pakistan border in the east, to the Turkish border in the northwest. The scale is overwhelming. From our location in Zahedan, we had the choice of two routes leading to the Iranian capital, Tehran. Both routes were former camel trails. The northerly route headed close to the Afghanistan border, and the sacred city of Mashed, then west skirting the Dasht-e-Kavïr salt flat, while the more southerly route meandered through the vast expanse of desert known as Dasht-e-Lût.

It may have been something as flippant as the toss of a coin, or the appealing names of the ancient towns, but we opted for the southern route. According to Dimitri, sand-drifts often obliterated this route, rendering people stranded for days. With a plume of dust in our wake, and carrying the optimum amount of water, we headed towards the arid wilderness of Dasht-e-Lût, where the dunes stretched all the way to the shimmering horizon.

This was a lonely road, with a hard, corrugated surface, and for the first time in miles, the speedometer nudged 50 mile per hour. With the engine now packing plenty of clout and producing an average speed of 40 mile per hour, we managed to establish a smooth run. After two hours of driving through the blistering sand, the sky turned grey. Gusts of wind howled across the landscape, filling the Jeep with sand from all angles as it snapped at the canopy.

Dasht-e-Lût.

With the Jeep slammed into four-wheel-drive, we ploughed over the drifts which were quickly consuming the road. Although we were wearing goggles, the intensity of the storm made it difficult to see, and the Jeep was soon up to its axles in sand. After about ten minutes, we scrambled over to a group of highway workers with a stationary lorry and with their help, began the tedious job of trying to release the Jeep. Once the axles were clear, Noel settled himself behind the steering wheel, then slipped the gears into four-wheel-drive until it clawed free.

Later that afternoon, we arrived in the eucalyptus-lined streets of Bam, where, in the short time it took us to buy a loaf, an armed police officer spotted the Jeep. In Iran, a visit to the local 'cop shop' usually equated with food, and Bam police station was no exception: while our documents were checked, we tucked in to tea and sticky cakes.

With the onset of dusk, the icy wind, and increasing altitude, the temperature began to plummet. We left Bam and headed back into the mountains. We hadn't anticipated this dynamic change in climate, and since it was almost impossible to drive, we stopped at the first opportunity to make camp: a cluster of boulders just off the road. Numb with cold and therefore incapable of lighting the stove, we bit into the loaf, punctured a hole in a soup tin, then drank the contents.

The wretched cold night spent wrapped in tropical-issue blankets was cut short by the clinking of animal harnesses and chattering Iranian tongues. Crawling from alongside the Jeep, we crouched silently behind the boulders as a phantom-like column of camels padded by.

'Too close for comfort.' Noel blew into his fist as they dissolved over the horizon. *'Half an hour later, they'd have spotted the Jeep in the early morning light.'*

The sun had already fractured the horizon revealing the dramatic Paye mountain range by 6.00 a.m. Snow-crowned Mount Alahezar and Häzärän, both over 14,000 feet, towered in the middle distance. Still numb and unable to sleep, we managed to light the hexamine stove, thaw out, then down several mess tins of tea, the first hot drink in over 24 hours.

The Jeep often refused to fire up on these cold mornings until the spark plugs had been heated over the flames of the hexamine. This particular morning was no exception, but after a dose of hot spark plugs, the engine burst into life.

Descending towards the village of Mahan, where we suppressed our hunger with lamb stew, sweetmeats and syrupy tea, the heat from the morning sun had already started to penetrate our lightweight clothes.

Leaving Mahan for Yazd, where the barren landscape was momentarily broken by a single tribe of nomads, the water-temperature gauge shot into the red. Wisps of steam curdling from beneath the engine cover confirmed the lower hose on the cooling system was leaking. A length of parachute cord wrapped around the damaged pipe, and secured with adhesive plaster, stemmed the leak, but it was nearly dusk by the time we'd completed this 'simple' repair.

Keeping a watchful eye on the temperature gauge, we continued through the night until we spotted an illuminated neon skyline – our first signpost for Yazd. The razor-sharp demarcation dividing the town from the desert gave the impression that Yazd was standing in its own grounds. With the exception of electric power little had changed since Marco Polo allegedly passed by in the 13th century: the old mosque, minarets and a mud-brick shops were all there.[3]

In the hope of receiving the usual warm, Iranian hospitality, we pre-empted a visit to Yazd police station, where we were offered accommodation, including a secure compound for the Jeep, in one of the police guesthouses. Lacking electricity and toilet facilities: a couple of cracked sinks in the backyard served as a communal bathroom, it soon became clear our ploy had backfired.

In these circumstances, we usually used our own water, along with the canvas bucket which made an ideal sink. Before going to bed this particular evening, I groped around in the dark, stopped up the plug-hole to one of the sinks with a piece of rag, and thinking little of the sticky, frogspawn substance lining the sink, began washing. The next morning when an elderly man relieved his phlegm-ridden lungs over the same basin, I realised it had previously been used as a spittoon.

'Hey, Mister, you want repair? I am Sayed, very good with engines.'

Showered in a cascade of welding sparks, a young mechanic picked his way towards us through a pile of spare parts and body panels. We were in a back street in the heart of Yazd where there were some 15 open-fronted, garage workshops.

'Yes, radiator and other work.' We showed Sayed the patched-up radiator hose, broken spring, and other miscellaneous faults.

'Going England? Very long way.' He continued looking over the Jeep.

'Engine mountings finished. Big job, much money.' Eyebrows and greasy palms raised to the heavens as if to say, *'Trust me, I'm an honest guy.'*

We knew the repairs, (including the engine, which had come away from the rubber mountings) would be time-consuming, but needed the work completed before leaving Yazd later in the afternoon. With the help of his guru Allah, Sayed was confident the Jeep would be ready before dusk; we settled on a price and left our fate in his hands.

On returning to the workshop later that afternoon, Sayed and a barefoot urchin were repairing the brakes, while another child was underneath the Jeep wielding a spanner.

'Sun no yet go down. Jeep nearly ready.' Sayed patted a greasy leather pouch around his waist oozing with bank notes.

By the time Sayed downed tools it was fast approaching dusk. He'd been unable to replace the headlamp because he didn't have a spare.

However, the engine mountings were now fixed, along with the spare-wheel bracket which had been welded back in place.

As we left Yazd the sun had almost vanished, leaving a slate-grey sky draining to the west. We skimmed along the corrugated road guided by the eye of one headlamp. For a while the moon cast a metallic burnish across the desert, then, as the clouds scuttled across the sky, a pall of black descended over the wilderness.

'It's gone 8.30 p.m., Noel.' The luminous dial on my watch picked out the time. *'Give it another half hour, then call it a day, shall we?'* I strained my eyes as the rod of anaemic light cast by the working headlamp probed the night.

'Yes, when you're ready, Roy.'

50 miles from Yazd, the engine began to misfire, making it increasingly difficult to keep the 'magic' 40 miles per hour, which gave a smooth run. A whiff of burnt rubber also laced the night air confirming more trouble with the cooling system.

Approaching Yazd.

Having been unable to buy replacement batteries for the torch, we were now reliant on the intermittent moonlight to look inside the engine, where we discovered a few drops of water around the bottom of the radiator. After the first refill, the radiator ran out of water quicker than we'd expected. Then the second time, it gushed out from the bottom as fast as it was poured in.

On closer inspection we could see that the short outlet pipe brazed to the radiator had fractured, partly pulled away, and in turn made an opening through which the water could escape. The hairline-crack in the severed joint causing the initial water loss, had been overlooked in the poor light. Aggravated by the terrain, the fracture was now clearly an open gap. After one more radiator fill-up, we'd need to use the water from the bottles in our survival kits.

'Looks like I'll be hitching to Qum with the radiator on my back.' Typically unflustered, Noel lit a cigarette while we considered what to do.

Hitching to the Qum, the nearest town, which was 200 miles away, seemed the only option. Given the infrequency of the traffic, a return hitch would take the best part of a day, so on the off chance there could be a village close by, we began to walk down the road. It was eerily silent, and the night sky was hanging like a sheet of black tarpaulin over the desert.

'What's that, listen?' Within less than ten minutes, Noel inclined his head to one side.

'Can't make it out.' We stared into the night, listening intently to a soft hissing sound, which became louder as we continued walking.

'Water!'

We ran towards the noise, and watched in disbelief as a stream meandered across the road between foam-flecked stones towards a couple of derelict stone huts and the remains of an excavation pit, (that may have originally served as a water basin) where we set up camp to shelter from the cold.

'Allow five hours to dry. Will fix most things; porcelain, wood....' Noel squinted at the small print on the tube of liquid metal. It seemed unlikely that this magic compound, with the dubious get-out clause of fixing *'most things,'* would be able to repair the radiator pipe, but we gave it our best shot.

There was still a collar of brazing around the pipe stub, from where it had pulled away from the radiator. Using this as a flange, we applied a coating

Preparing breakfast in the excavation pit.
The damaged radiator is in the foreground.

of liquid metal to the brazing, then impacted the pipe back in place. Once the pipe seemed relatively secure, we covered a piece of gauze with the remaining liquid metal, fashioned it around the pipe and fracture, shaped it up to the radiator, then left it to dry.

Shivering with cold, and eager to see the results of our experiment, the next morning we were up before dawn. Much to our relief, after refitting, and filling the radiator with water, it didn't leak. With all the water vessels filled from the spring, we broke camp and headed for the Shiite pilgrim city of Qum, where later that afternoon, we purchased fuel and fur gloves, before heading for the Iranian capital, Tehran.

When the Damâvand mountain, dominating Tehran's skyline came into view, the sweet buzz of the tyres on tarmac gave a momentary sense of relief as the mileometer touched 50 miles per hour, but in the split-second we'd been distracted by the impressive Damâvand, the Jeep veered across the road to the edge of an embankment. Minutes later we were attending a puncture. This time, the inner tube of the offending wheel had been reduced to shreds, but with the benefit of a decent road surface, plus our significant experience, we changed the wheel in pit-stop time.

The Arabic signposts littering the crowded, metropolitan dust bowl of Tehran were impossible to decipher, and as we drove aimlessly through the streets trying to pick up a northwest road, we were pulled up by a police officer. Assuming we were a higher rank than himself, the officer constantly addressed us as 'Sir' and offered to guard the Jeep while we went for something to eat. It was an ideal arrangement.

From Tehran, we traced the foothills of the snow-capped Alborz mountains framing the southerly bowl of the Caspian Sea, making an early camp in a shack, somewhere in the region of Qazvin.[4] This was a poignant benchmark in that it was two months since we'd left Singapore. While calculating for breakdowns and diffiicult terrain, we'd expected to complete the journey in this time, but we were still 4,000 miles from home. The consequence of being about a month behind schedule had a significant impact on everything from finances to food. Due to a shortage of warm, waterproof clothes, we were also unprepared for the forthcoming winter conditions.

Shortly after breaking camp the next day, we made our first navigational error. In part this was due to a complete lack of signposts and inadequate maps. An Iranian driver, who we flagged down while trimming the weight in the back of the Jeep to compensate for a broken spring, confirmed our mistake; we were 15 miles off course, heading for Iraq, instead of Turkey. Looping back, we found a garage in Zanjan to replace the broken spring with the spare, and braze the fractured radiator which had started to leak again.

Later that evening, shouldering the slopes of Mount Sahand, we bedded down alongside a pile of tools and used coffee cups, in a worker's hut adjacent to a quarry. Plans to leave the hut in advance of any workers arriving the following day, were disbanded, when we were awoken by the sound of approaching footsteps - we'd clearly overslept. With just seconds to spare, we grabbed our boots, flung open the door and declared,

'Good Morning!'

Camping close to the Azerbaijan frontier.

Six workmen, already armed with lengths of timber, stared in disbelief as we volunteered a welcoming handshake. Amused by our antics (fortunately, they quickly understood we'd only used the hut for a bedroom), we enlisted their help to tow start the Jeep, which again had a flat battery, then with thanks all round,headed through the mountains towards Tabriz.

That evening we took refuge from the sleet and impending gale-force winds by securing the custom-made tent over the remaining four walls of a derelict stone hut close to the Azerbaijan frontier. Protected from the elements, we sat late into the night trying to repair the petrol cooking stove, which in producing intermittent flames had made it impossible to cook.

Ensuring the tank was filled with cheap petrol, we reached the heavily guarded frontier post of Bazargan. A spectacular view of Mount Ararat, the alleged resting place of Noah's Ark, dominated the horizon. Turkey was just a hop over the fence.

Endnotes

[1] 65 miles from the border with Iran.

[2] In intense heat, petrol may vaporise in the fuel pump, and cause fuel starvation.

[3] Yazd was formerly the hub of Zoroastrianism, a dualistic religion, for which one of the fundamental practices is to expose the deceased in purpose-built towers, to be picked clean by vultures.

[4] The fortified castle remains belonging to the 11th century Hashishiyun cult are in a remote valley near to Qazvin/Ghazivin. Under the influence of hashish, the Hashishiyuns despatched their 'hit men' on suicide missions to murder leading political and religious figures in the region. They believed their suicide missions would lead them to paradise, where they would be received by beautiful maidens. The Mongols overthrew the Hashishiyuns in the 12th century.

CHAPTER 8

MILK & MONEY

Mount Ararat.
Snow-capped and majestic.

CHAPTER 8

MILK & MONEY

'Do you have a criminal record? Are you carrying any illegal currency? Have you a firearm? Have you ever suffered from Tuberculosis? Do you have Tuberculosis? Is your mind sound? Is your vehicle insured?'

We gave impartial answers to the questions on the Turkish immigration form, crossed the frontier, then headed due north through an area of barren steppeland towards Erzurum. The raw wind cut through our clothes, freezing us to the bone, yet for all this, we were awe struck by the sheer scale of the terrain. Looking back across the steppes towards Iran, Mount Ararat, snow-capped and majestic, peaked through the clouds, in the bleakest of landscapes.

Guided by the one working headlight, we made reasonable progress through the fog and gentle snowfall, but when darkness fell, visibility became so impaired, we had to crawl along on what we hoped, was the correct track.

'Pull up Roy, a checkpoint.'

A group of armed soldiers brandishing flashlights emerged out of the fog and directed us into the guardroom where we were confronted by a military police officer – a taciturn figure sporting a felted, handlebar moustache and immaculate uniform

'You've trespassed into a prohibited military zone.' A cloying,Turkish accent overpowered his near-perfect command of English.

'It was unintentional, it's almost impossible to see in the fog. Is it far from here to Erzurum?' We bailed out our excuses.

'About 25 miles.' He snapped, irritated by our insouciance. *'You are foreign nationals without a government permit, and have illegally entered a sensitive military area. This is a serious offence in Turkey.'*

Synchronising his watch with the guardroom clock, he rattled off sections of Turkish military law, copied particulars from our documents into his incident book, then telephoned through to the brigade commander. Minutes later, we were escorted to a concrete bunker where a group of soldiers were engrossed around a three-dimensional model landscape. There was an eerie atmosphere about this place: the hum of the generator, the crackling communication system and an anaemic light filtering through a warren of corridors.

'Mr Dudgeon, Mr Follows, please take a seat.' Our names ricocheted between the walls as the brigade commander stepped forward.

'I understand you don't have a government permit allowing you to drive directly to Ankara through the military zone?'

'Correct.' Noel and I appeased in unison.

'This time we have decided to believe you. We will allow you to continue your journey, but the penalty for entering this military zone without a permit will mean taking the considerably longer, mountain road to Istanbul. It's about 300 miles. Understand?'

We nodded in agreement. This wasn't the time for negotiating, and although we didn't have the appropriate clothing or equipment for the freezing conditions, we'd expected a more rigorous sentence.

The commander continued, *'To see you through the military checkpoints, one of my men will accompany you as far as Erzurum, where you'll stay the night. Then as you are not allowed to go west through the military zone, you will make your way north to the Black Sea port of Trabzon. Take care, the weather is often treacherous in this mountainous region.'* He picked out the area on our map.

'From Trabzon you will continue west along the coast road for 300 miles to Samsun, then drive inland for 275 miles until you reach Ankara.' He made it sound so easy.

A young soldier wearing a balaclava and greatcoat joined us in the Jeep. Although he spoke just a smattering of English, we established a rapport, passed swiftly through two military checkpoints, then checked into a hotel in Erzurum as pre-arranged. Having survived on tinned sardines and stale chappattis for the last few days, our priority now was to find food.

The next day, after cleaning out the petrol pump,we drove northwest to a final military checkpoint, left our escort, then picked up a cart track which touched on part of the Old Silk Road. This was wolf country, a wild and desolate landscape leading to the snow-tipped Kirklir Mountains, where colourless patches of vegetation and skeletal trees struggled to survive.

Gentle snowfall on the way to Erzurum.

With the ever-increasing altitude, the delicate snowfall turned into a savage blizzard, forcing drifts of snow around the foot pedals of the Jeep, which we had to dig away. The Jeep continued skidding in four-wheel-drive, and consequently it took over four hours to drive the 67 miles to Bayburt, a bleak spot, 4,000 feet above sea level. Failing to persuade a couple of villagers to allow us to take refuge in their cattle shed, we were obliged to continue to the Black Sea, Byzantine port of Trabzon. Five hours later, as we thawed out in a guesthouse overlooking the Black Sea, the perilous blizzard which had encrusted the Jeep with snow, was just a dream.

Replenished with food, sleep and warmth, from Trabzon we traced the loop of road around the secluded bays of the Yasin Burnu peninsula, where bright-coloured caïques lay washed-up on the sand. From Samsun, the last bay, we aimed inland towards the foot of the Egerli Mountains, where the cellar of a derelict stone hut camouflaged in a coppice of woodland provided a dry shelter for the night.

With plans to reach Ankara before dark, we broke camp early, and within a couple of hours were in the foothills of the snowy Egerli mountains, attending to a lorry driver who'd veered off the road.

Our delayed arrival in Ankara was brought about by a flat tyre which proved difficult to change with cold hands, stopping in Sungurlu, to have the inner tube repaired, and thaw out over several bowls of goulash. With the banks in Ankara now closed, and insufficient lira to buy much-needed petrol and food, we persuaded a taxi driver to take us to a black-market

The Yasin Burnu peninsula.

currency exchange. In sharp contrast to many other countries Turkey generally accepted traveller's cheques, but there were stringent penalties for trading on the vibrant black market. With these thoughts in mind, we followed the taxi through the back streets of Ankara to a milk bar: a most unlikely place to be trading on the black market.

In the foothills of the Egerli Mountains.
Above: Noel Dudgeon
Below: Roy Follows. Note the fur gloves.

Once we'd paid the taxi driver with the last of our liras, he slipped through a beaded fly-curtain to fetch 'The Boss,' a taurine figure, pummelling a fist of worry beads.

'I hear you want to do business. You know the consequences if caught. How much you have sell and what price?' Given his occupation, he wasn't the fluffy puss we'd anticipated. Noel, in his best attempt to appear confident, came straight to the point, but was quickly rebuked.

That's chicken shit. I was told you had plenty money to sell, you're wasting my time.' Pussy was ready to pounce.

'*We also have sterling and US dollars in cash, but will only sell along with the traveller's cheques.'* Noel broke in to pacify.

'You make conditions? Pussy shot a glance at his henchmen. 'I'll buy dollars and traveller's but no Ingleesh pounds.' Looping the worry beads around his wrist, he counted the notes and traveller's cheques placed on the table, then peeled off the money due, from a wad of Turkish lira inside his jacket.

Suspecting the two henchmen who'd observed this amicable, but strained transaction, may try to steal our recently acquired cash, we declined a complimentary glass of milk, discreetly walked outside, then ran to the Jeep. Seconds later, when the henchmen came running from the bar, the warm engine was already fired up, and we pulled away in the nick of time.

To minimise expenses, that evening we camped beneath a low bridge on the outskirts Ankara, which due to the imposed curfew, was free of traffic. We soon fell asleep after rustling up an 'all-in'[1] but at some unearthly hour in the morning, thundering lorries crossing just a few feet above our heads, followed by falling debris, made for an early start. After a quick brew, we headed for the ferry terminal on the Bosphorus Strait where vessels from every nation swung at anchor.

Skimmed by a halo of seagulls, the ferry eased into the lead-coloured Bosphorus. Looking back from the stern as we butted across the Golden Horn towards Istanbul, Asia faded away in the misty rain. Suddenly the prospect of reaching England seemed realistic.

Driving through Istanbul's crowded waterfront where a confusion of foreign tongues plied their trade, and Christian churches rubbed shoulders with bulbous mosques, a young man poked his greasy head inside the Jeep to deliver a super-sales pitch.

'Psst! psst! Johnny want Spanish fly or dirty postcards?'

Failing to accept a polite 'no,' when rebuked with some choice expletives, he then danced about, threatening the wrath of Allah.

'To minimise expenses we camped beneath a low bridge on the outskirts of Ankara.'

Later that afternoon, having failed to secure visas from Istanbul's Yugoslav Embassy, we contemplated our next move from the lofty room of a threadbare guesthouse. In the eyes of the hard line embassy staff, visas had been refused on the grounds of our employment status, *'Police Officer, Malayan Police Force'* confirmed on the application. In short, we'd inadvertently admitted to being engaged in anti-Communist activity. To add insult to injury, the Yugoslavs had also withheld our passports. Forced to seek advice from Istanbul's British consulate, the severity of the event secured an immediate invitation to the home of the British Ambassador to Turkey, where we outlined the facts over tea and sandwiches.

Following a heated telephone conversation with his Yugoslav counterpart, the Ambassador clinched the release of our passports, however the Yugoslav's wouldn't concede to issuing visas. Without the authority to override this decision, the British ambassador had proposed we applied for visas at the Yugoslav Consul in Thessalonika, Greece. This was a long shot, but we were hoping to foil the Yugoslavs by entering innocuous job descriptions on the visa application.

The following day, before collecting the Jeep and heading 150 miles north to Edirne, the Turkish frontier that butts onto Greece, we wandered through the vaulted labyrinth of Istanbul's Grand Bazaar. Wailing Arabic music competed with Western tunes from a bank of loudspeakers as the traders plied their smooth, hypnotic patter to seal the fate of the most reticent passer-by. Determined not to succumb to any sales patter, when prompted by an Aladdin-like character to buy a couple of bearskin coats, we reversed the sales pitch, and sold him our binoculars.

With the Jeep defective steering, broken spring, handbrake and headlights, now repaired, our next priority was to ensure the Edirne border guards didn't notice the currency discrepancy in our passports.

To create confusion, we'd added extra papers to the bona fide document file, and worked a ruse to feign petrol was leaking from the Jeep. We could also capitalise on being 'brother' police officers, since Turkey and Malaya were primarily Moslem countries.

Confident our well-rehearsed plans would prove sufficiently distracting, we arrived at the Edirne border, shook hands with our 'brother' police officers, then began the routine task of checking paperwork. Everything seemed to be going to plan, until Noel, with an urgency in his voice that wasn't in our script shouted;

'*Quick Roy, there's petrol leaking.*' Following Noel outside, I jack-knifed from my seat, spilling tea down my shirt.

'No smoking. Put out cigarettes! Put out cigarettes!'

The hardstanding around the Jeep was glistening with fuel: the tap allowing fuel to pass from the long-range tanks into the main, had somehow worked loose, or not been properly closed off.

Two stationary lorries reversed to a safer spot, while the staff flapped about looking for buckets and a fire extinguisher. This genuine fire hazard caused more confusion than anything we could have planned, and consequently we slipped into Greece with a wad of undeclared currency.

Faced with a leaking radiator hose that was impossible to repair in the failing light, that evening we slept in an empty garage on the compound at the Greek frontier. In the light of day, the radiator was impossible to repair without the expertise of a mechanic, so as a temporary measure, we ensured both jerry cans were full of water for regular 'top-ups.'

From the Greek border we headed south for Alexandropolis, tracing the Aegean coastline due west through pine woods and olive groves. From the high vantage point of the coastal road blue breakers crashed onto the rocks and sun-bleached shore. Sometimes the road turned inland passing through timeless villages, where strings of donkeys jogged freely along the narrow, rutted streets. With a tranquillity that belied the region's turbulent past, both spires and minarets are prevalent in many of the villages, giving rise to Greece's remarkable, although often strained, multiculturalism.

From Xanthi, where the cobbled streets meandered through the charismatic old Turkish quarter, the road headed back towards the coast and port of of Kavála through a patchwork of tobacco and sunflower fields. Vibrant-coloured boats were unloading their catch, next to the snack bar where we encouraged the proprietor to exchange some dollars into much-needed drachmas. Having lost track of the days, the significance of being given two chocolate eggs as we left the bar wasn't immediately apparent, but it was infact, Easter Sunday.

60 miles on, where the forrested road along the Aegean shoreline headed inland, we passed an English couple who'd run out of fuel. The first vehicle they'd seen in hours, they couldn't believe we had fuel to spare. Once their engine had been replenished with a full jerry can, they continued their tour of Greece, but ironically, in the short time we'd stopped to help, the Jeep's battery went flat. Unable to fire-up the engine, the Jeep had to be pushed up the incline of the road, then free-wheeled down the other side until the engine burst into life.

The cultural melting pot of Thessalonika, the second city of Greece, was our last opportunity to secure Yugoslav visas. We stayed in a simple hotel within walking distance from the Yugoslav Consulate, and that evening discussed our 'visa tactics' over a few beers in a local bar. Common sense should have prevailed for an early night, but we happened to raise the curiosity of a table of celebrating Greeks. Drinking arrack cocktails at such a rate, their infectious party atmosphere meant our plans for an early night went out of the window.

Above: Istanbul's Grand Bazaar.
'We reversed the sales pitch and sold him our binoculars.'

Below: Radiator repairs, at the Athens Express garage, Thessalonika.

The next morning we entered the Yugoslav Consulate feeling nauseous and hung over. Hoping the staff hadn't been alerted by their colleagues in Istanbul, we handed our passports to a truculent civil servant.

'English?' He snapped over the pages, then reluctantly shoved a couple of visa application forms across the desk.

This time, we confirmed our employment status as 'dustman' and following a tense three hour wait, the passports were endorsed with the obligatory rubber stamp.

Before crossing into Yugoslavia, the radiator was repaired with a 'quick-fix' liquid sealant at the Athens Express garage: a more permanent repair involved brazing the water channels and was beyond our budget, then filled up with petrol, which was rationed over the border.

Endnotes

[1] 'All-in' See Appendix I. Page 192.

ALL COMMUNICATIONS WITH MEMBERS ARE CONFIDENTIAL AND MUST NOT BE
TELEPHONE 31016 & 31017
THE AUTOMOBILE
MEMBER OF THE ALLIANCE INTERNATIONALE DE TOURISME,
AFFILIATED WITH THE ROYAL
K. G. BURNE
Secretary and Treasurer,
Y. W. CHAN
Asst. Secretary
PLEASE QUOTE
OUR REF.
S&G/F
S.R.Follows,Esq.,
Marine Police H.Q.,
Tampoi,
Johore.
Dear Sir,
Many thanks for your letter
enclosing $12.50 in payment of your
Association. Your prompt attention in
much appreciated, and our official
membership card have been despatched to
cover.
It is noted that you have
the overland trip from Singapore to the
and Burma, and we shall deem it a favour
a brief account of the journey performed
our Highway magazine. Your experience
will no doubt be found most invaluable
Association wishing to contemplate such
Y.W.CHAN
Automobile
SINGAPORE
S10486

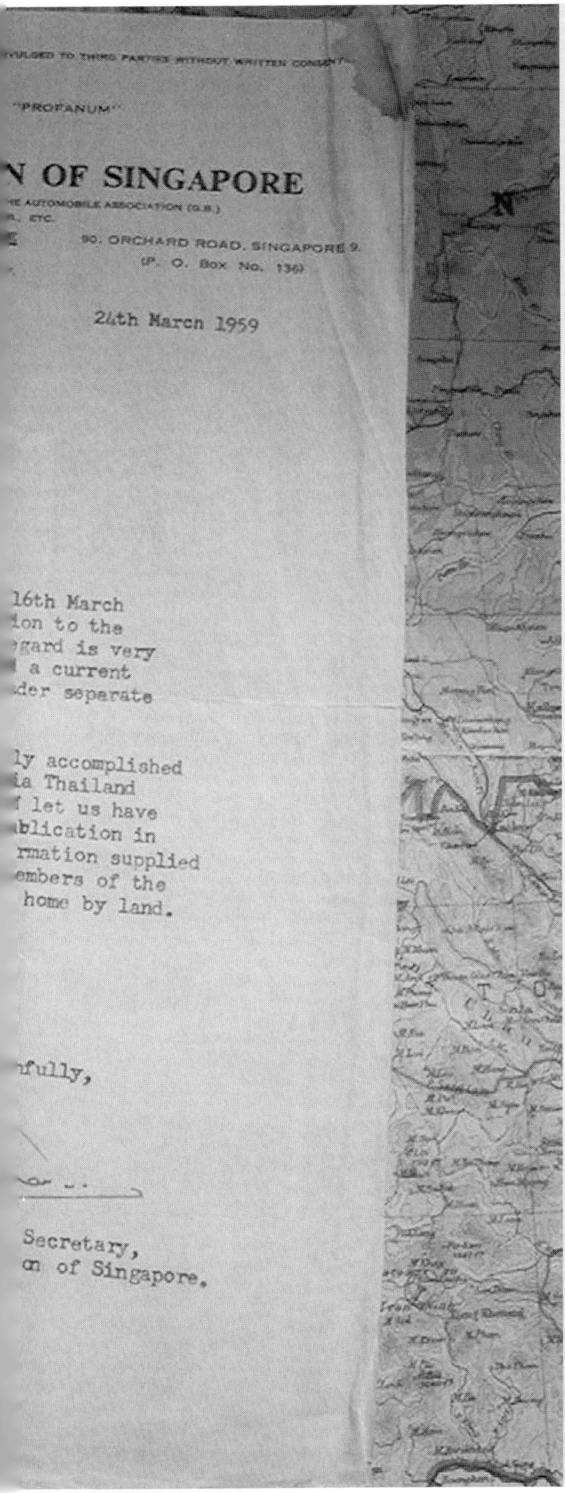

CHAPTER 9

MUDDY NUMBERS

Letter from the Singapore Automobile Association along with the original membership badge.

We joined the Singapore AA simply to acquire a badge, but never enlisted their help, since most of the places where the Jeep brokedown were too remote.

CHAPTER 9

MUDDY NUMBERS

From the Greek border we crossed the short frontier tract into Yugoslavia. A dishevelled soldier raised the barrier pole and jerked his thumb towards the border control 'office,' a fortified bunker with several armoured vehicles parked outside and a cluster of antennas on the roof. Inside, a group of officials were silently shuffling papers behind a glass screen. A flaccid-looking clerk with a counterfeit smile pushed open the window hatch.

'So what your work in Malaya?' He ran a finger inside his shirt collar and scrutinised our documents for a flaw, or reason to create one. From the barred window facing onto the road, we could just make out three soldiers inspecting the Jeep. We were in for a grilling.

When asked our state of employment, we again confirmed we were dustmen, and two hours later, our passports were given the stamp of approval allowing us to officially enter Yugoslavia, but there was just one hitch and he was trotting towards the Jeep waving a fistful of papers.

'Stop! Stop! I'm the Manager for The Health and Safety Enforcement Department.'

We were unaware that health and safety regulations imposed by the Yugoslav Government qualified the Jeep as a potential health hazard. For all the frontiers we'd crossed this was a first. The irony of Tito's presidency meant there was a shortage of soap and toiletries, but gallons of disinfectant to clean innocuous vehicles.

The concrete 'decontamination trough' contained a rusty, effluent-smelling liquid, with a crust of debris floating on the surface. Indifferent to the fact that the contents of the trough were likely to be toxic, the 'Decontamination Manager' stood anxiously with pen and notepad in hand, prompting Noel to drive through. While Noel eased the Jeep into the trough, I was reprimanded for trying to take photographs so, to avoid being interned on a collective potato farm, quickly put away the camera.

We headed out on a northerly road following the River Varda through the mountains towards Skopje where the cold began to bite as we hit a blizzard which filled the Jeep with snow. The goggles only marginally improved visibility which was reduced to less than six feet. Our late arrival in Skopje meant the city was deserted. Desperate to find somewhere to sleep, we pulled up at the first sign offering accommodation, where the congenial proprietor made up for the modest surroundings: dimly lit, with cheap, veal-coloured, linoleum flooring, this small hotel was a far cry from the Hilton.

'Now, I need your passports, driving licences, any other proof of identity, and you'll both need to complete one of these four-page questionnaires.' His eyebrows peaked in disapproval. I'm so sorry about all this paperwork.'

'We're only staying the night, not buying the place.' We teased, browsing through the pages of complex questions.

'Unfortunately it's central Government orders. All foreign nationals must complete the form.' He smiled, appreciating the torment.

At the time, most, if not all the hotels in Yugoslavia were state-controlled. The room prices were therefore non-negotiable, and on booking a room, it was compulsory to complete a government-issue questionnaire. After we'd penned in our ambiguous replies, the manager produced a couple of glasses and a bottle of home-made plum brandy from underneath the reception desk. Countless refills later, we staggered along the hotel corridor in search of our room.

The next day, we headed north-east through the Morava Valley, to Belgrade. From Christian-dominated Skopje, we passed through the Moslem town of Kumanovo, which was still bound by historic traditions from some 500 years of Ottoman domination. Moving further north towards Nis, and the hub of a complex religious order, where the simmering tensions between neighbouring sects had yet to erupt, and in the early 1990s, conclude in Yugoslavia's devolution.

From Kumanovo, our next port of call was the industrial town of Nis, where even the birds looked unhappy.[1] 80 miles from Nis the road improved, and although the brakes were still defective, we clutched onto the side of the Jeep and rattled along at over 50 miles per hour. It was not yet midday, so with 175 miles to go, and sufficient petrol, we were well on target to reach Belgrade before dark.

On approaching Belgrade, the surrounding forestry dotted with wooden huts gave way to oppressive industrial sprawl, until we drove through the main boulevard of imposing, grey buildings, statues and monuments. For all its grandeur, Belgrade was sombre, and the locals appeared melancholic as they scurried about in their uniform fur hats.

Communist Yugoslavia was not the place for two Colonial police officers to relax, and to avoid attracting the attention of anyone in uniform we immediately pulled up alongside a group of young people and asked directions to the British Embassy. Delighted and curious to speak with two Englishmen, it was handshakes all round, and well over half an hour before they finally came to giving us directions.

Paddy, a mutual friend, (and former Malay police officer), assigned to the British Embassy in Belgrade, was aware of our trip, but didn't know when we'd be driving through Yugoslavia. After some initial enquiries, we tracked him down; he was off duty in the Embassy club house.

No! I don't believe it. I'd given you up!' Paddy slapped Noel and I on the

Noel & Paddy outside the British Embassy, Belgrade.

back. *'What the hell delayed you?'* He ribbed, shaking our hands in disbelief.

'Nothing really, just the odd hiccup here and there.' Noel understated.

'Knowing you two, I bet it was. Anyway, congratulations on reaching Belgrade, you deserve a drink.' Paddy ordered a round of drinks and introduced us to his friends.

Our visit to the British Embassy was timely, since Paddy and his friends briefed us about the complexities of the People's Republic: it was clear that although we'd been allowed into Yugoslavia, our departure was not guaranteed.

Given this advice, and our previous experience of Yugoslav protocol, we decided to stay in Belgrade for just one night, and that evening, were kindly put up in the comfort of Paddy's home. Returning to the British Embassy Club after dinner with Paddy and his wife, we outlined our concerns about driving through Yugoslavia to Austria. Our finances, a mix of sterling and traveller's cheques, was sufficient to see us to England, on the grounds that we wouldn't have to pay for any Jeep repairs. Petrol rationing also posed a problem in that we were unable to establish if petrol was available along the 345- mile route to the Yugoslav-Austrian frontier. Fortunately, Paddy came to the rescue with a quota of petrol coupons he didn't need.

Thanking Paddy and his friends, we left Belgrade with a full tank of fuel and repaired brakes. Heading first for Zagreb, then the Hungarian-Austrian border of Varazdin, instead of making camp, which may have attracted unwanted attention, we chanced our luck in a small café from where the perfumed smell of Balkan tobacco filtered into the street. The waitress directed us to a bed-and-breakfast, where much to our delight, after all the form-filling,the owner cooked a midnight supper.

The following morning, we drove 60 miles from Varazdin to the Yugoslav–Austrian frontier. We were the only travellers at the border control and, therefore anxious that we may be subject to a full scrutiny by the Yugoslav border guards.

A soldier dressed in greatcoat and fur hat stepped from the sentry box and pointed his rifle in the direction of the frontier office. Here, a young army officer went through the familiar paperwork and with typical Communist dogma, asked to see our WHO [2] inoculation certificates.

'Strange!' The young officer flashed, arching his eyebrows. *'Travelled all the way from Singapore, yet only stayed a couple of nights in the People's Republic. Your documents, passports, and how much money are you carrying?'*

To justify our 'short stay' we gave the impression of not having sufficient money, and didn't present all our traveller's cheques or sterling currency.

In contrast, we were processed through the Austrian border post in minutes.

We expected the 'home run' from Austria to England to be relatively free of problems, but shortly outside the Austrian border post, the nearside front wheel suffered a puncture which sent the Jeep skating across the road, and shredded the inner tube. With the spare wheel fitted, we laboured through the snow-filled mountain passes of the eastern Alps to Salzburg.

Unaware, the green, army boiler suits we'd had on all day, were at all conspicuous, in the brief moment we entered a bar in the heart of Salzburg, a couple of Austrians, who'd clearly overindulged on the schnaps, walked over to Noel. *'You German military?'*

The Yugoslav-Austrian border post.

Yes, 53rd Jaeger Division.' Almost by reflex, Noel drew himself up, and looked straight into the Austrian's bloodshot eyes. Hours later, we all stumbled into the street, shook hands and went our respective ways.

Despite the luxury of sleeping beneath continental quilts, which we experienced in Salzburg for the first time, we awoke with thumping hangovers. Reluctantly, we left the comfort of our beds to find a garage to fit new inner tubes. Still feeling rough, it was midday by the time we left Salzburg.

We sailed through the Austrian-German frontier, then joined a decent road through part of the Alps, maintaining a reasonable speed to Munich. Then it was on through Bavaria, Stuttgart and Baden-Baden, where we risked the expense and stayed in a decent hotel. Eager to move on, the next morning we were up before dawn, but it took over an hour of tinkering with the engine, plus the help of a passer-by, before we were up and

Petrol stop, Austria.

running.

We arrived at our last foreign frontier before England, the German-French border control, then crossed the Rhine to Strasbourg, and on into France. By mid-afternoon we were crossing the Champagne-Ardennes, heading for Paris, our ninth capital city. It was turning dusk when to the amazement of taxis and traffic police, we rattled through the Arc de Triomphe, and down the Champs Elysées.

Later in the evening, having exchanged the last of our traveller's cheques for an excellent rate, with a couple of American merchant bankers in a restaurant, we hailed a taxi, and sped off into the night declaring, *'Wine, women and song – the best night club in town!'*

For all its seductive lighting, waiters in penguin suits, and female singer prowling between cocktail-covered tables, this favoured Parisian nightclub wasn't really our type of place, but we still managed to stay until the early hours. The privilege of drinking in this premier location, only became apparent when we received the bill, which far exceeded our budget. Highly embarrassed, we volunteered to wash glasses, clean the toilets - anything to pay our way, but were merely cursed by the manager, before being released into the night, without even having to fold a napkin.

The next day, at both Boulogne and Calais, we missed the last ferry crossing. Determined to set foot on English soil, from Calais we sped across to Dunkirk, catching the 2.00 a.m. ferry with just minutes to spare. There was only a handfull of passengers on board, one of whom, relayed a graphic account of her 'epic drive' from Nice to Dunkirk until the white cliffs of Dover ghosted into view.

We'd been away from England for over three years, and were longing to set our eyes on this famous English coastline. With the aid of a tug, the ferry gently nosed into its berth, where the regular throb of the engine weakened to a slow, dying pulse. Before we knew it, we'd driven down the ramp into the disembarking area. In the brief moment we stopped to read a confusion of signs, a contemptuous voice yelled,

'Hey, have you two anything to declare?' We were clearly back in England.

Nothing at all.'

'No cigarettes or spirits?'

No, Sir.'

'No Antiquities, rugs, gemstones...?' He droned on.

We believed our declaration was honest; antiquities and rugs – we weren't even carrying enough money to buy our allowance of spirits and cigarettes from the duty-free shop.

Disappointed at not finding any contraband in our luggage, the customs official began to rummage through the Jeep. Meticulous in the extreme, he checked every nook and cranny, including the inside of the blackened kettle. There was nothing incriminating inside the Jeep, but on turning his head to dismiss us, he caught sight of the camera, dangling by its strap from the roof support.

'What's this, then? Evading duty on a camera? I think we'd better go to the office and sort this lot out.' His chest inflated with joy.

'A German camera ...expensive.' He slipped the camera from its shoddy case. I'd purchased the camera in duty-free Singapore, shortly after joining the Malay Police. For all the frontiers we'd crossed, it had never been a point of issue.

'How much was this? And the receipt? Where's the receipt?'

Desperate to exert his authority, he produced a booklet showing the serial numbers and prices of all the well-known makes of camera. By comparing serial numbers, he could establish the cost of purchasing a duplicate camera in England. This was considerably more than the price paid for the camera in Singapore: if he'd asked, we could have told him this information, and saved him the effort of consulting his little book.

Failing to appeal to the compassionate side of his nature - he was aware that we were carrying less than £15.00 in cash, we were given the 'choice' of leaving the camera in a bond until I returned to Malaya, or paying £15.00 duty. With no other choice but to leave the camera, we lost the once-in-a-lifetime opportunity of taking photographs to mark the end of the journey. If only we'd taken his name.

To ensure the camera would be returned before I set sail for Malaya, we demanded a receipt along with details on how to retrieve it. In hindsight, if he hadn't been so elated to score with the camera, he would have noticed my watch.

Deflated, we turned out of the docks onto the main road, past a police officer wobbling along on a bicycle. Surprised to see the Jeep, he momentarily forgot he was on two wheels, and almost fell off. Once he regained his composure, he frantically blasted his whistle for us to stop. Noel applied the brakes, but it took some distance before we came to a halt. Desperate to catch up, his legs pumped away at the pedals like pistons. Red in the face, with his helmet askew, he pulled up alongside the Jeep.

'So lads, what do we have here then? Muddy number plates with a strange registration?' Eyebrows knitted together, note-pad and pencil poised.

'It's Malayan, Sir.'

'Malayan. Please may I see you're driving licences and insurance certificate?' He was the polite, old-school copper, in his fifties.

'Everything's here Sir. Licences, carnet, passports, the lot.' We handed him our document file.

'Ah yes, Colonial Police, Malaya. That's interesting. You've been fighting the Mau Mau. I've read all about your force, you're doing a good job.'

Noel shot me a meaningful glance. The Mau Mau were terrorists in Kenya, but we didn't have the nerve to correct him. Hinting that we had lots to do in London, we pressed on.

'Half past eight! That's gone quick. He glanced at his pocket watch. *It's been good speaking to you lads, but take a tip from me, clean that rear number plate before reaching the big smoke – the cops up there aren't like us.'*

Police HQ in Malaya had agreed, that on arriving in London we'd collect the money due from the Crown Agents for the Colonies. The Crown Agents however were unaware of the arrangement. Declining to return home and outline our request in writing, the junior civil servant passed the buck to his superior, who began to wade through our documents with meticulous precision.

'Everything looks in order to me, but what about bills for petrol, food, incidentals - all the wining and dining. The luxury hotels...'

We'd been in England for less than five hours, but already the camera had been confiscated in Dover, we'd been pulled up by the police, and now the Crown Agencies were demanding to see a receipt book.

'Sometimes you slept under the stars, even sold your socks. I see.' He chewed the top of his pen in contemplation, as we described the 'luxury' peepshow hotel in Rangoon, trading fags for food - the world beyond his leafy Berkshire home, which didn't need receipts to function.

Given the Jeep's headlights were out of order, by the time he'd conceded to our 'exceptional case,' we were obliged to stay overnight in London, the tenth, and final capital city of the journey.

The next morning we headed north along the A34 towards Stoke-on-Trent, and four hours later pulled up outside The George Hotel in Burslem. Waiting outside, immaculately dressed, with the usual fragrance about her, was my fiancée, Doris. It was good to be home at last.

'Something hidden. Go and find it. Go and look behind the ranges -
Something lost behind the ranges. Lost and waiting for you. Go!

The Explorer.
Rudyard Kipling.

Endnotes

[1] Nis was seized by the Turks in 1386, and again in 1433. In 1809, when Stevan Sindjelich and 3,000 Serbian insurgents were killed in combat, the Turkish commandant of Nis, hoping to strike fear in the hearts of the people ordered the skulls of the killed Serbs, to be used in building a tower known as Chele-Kula. Today, Chele-Kula is a place of pilgrimage for the Serbs.

[2] World Health Organisation.

EPILOGUE

After celebrating over a few drinks at The George, Noel drove the Jeep to his home in Blackburn, where later that month it was sold to a farmer. The money due from the Crown Agents for the Colonies was also paid into our bank accounts.

The overland journey had consumed most of my leave, and I'd been home for less than a week, when I received notification regarding the renewal of my three-year contract with the Malay Police. Normally, I would have immediately signed and returned the papers, then waited several weeks before receiving the confirmation date of my return passage. This time I was reticent; I'd been involved in a 'telegram-and-letter' courtship for several years.

Doris and I had always lived in the same locality. As a boy my newspaper round took me to the family home, we attended the same schools, and during National Service, I served in the same army unit as her brother. Despite all these close connections, we only vagely knew each other.

On one occasion, when I was on leave, I happened, (although I never mastered the art), to go to the local dance-hall, where we struck up conversation. It soon became apparent we were not complete strangers, thereafter we became 'an item,' albeit separated by half the world with my obligations in Malaya.

With just a few weeks to spare before returning to Malaya, Doris agreed to marry, so my renewal documents were completed with the proviso of requiring an additonal passage. Accepting the only available date from our local registry office, after a small, family wedding, we headed for London to arrange passports and innoculations for my wife.

Two weeks later, we were departing from Liverpool Docks on the SS Menelaus, a Blue Funnel Line, cargo ship. This was only her second voyage, and everything on board was of the highest quality, and brand new. By virtue of being a cargo vessel, the handful of passenger cabins, or 'staterooms,' were opulent. There was also a disproportionate number of crew to passengers, so the service was exceptional.

While the cargo was being loaded, a customs official came on board and returned the camera. It was in fine working order, but the film, had been removed.

Several days into the voyage, on entering the turbulant Bay of Biscay, the ship began to roll. The listing was so severe, the fruit bowl on the cabin table was sent flying.

With the ship pitching from port to starboard, my wife was gripped by acute seasickness, which remained intermittent throughout the voyage. Three years in the Merchant Navy had possibly rendered me immune, so with the overland journey fresh in my mind, I put pen to paper.

On arriving in Malaya, I quickly settled into the rhythm of things at Marine Police HQ in Johore, and my wife soon learnt Malay. 18 months later I received notice of a dream job, a transfer to Penang, the 'Pearl of the Orient.' This was before the advent of tourism, so at our home near Batu Ferringhi beach, and on the adjacent islands of Langkawi and Pangkor, there were always more palms than people.

APPENDIX I

PLANNING.

In advance of embarking on a journey of this magnitude, it's essential to plan ahead. One of the key points is to base the departure date around forthcoming seasonal hazards. For example, when arriving in Burma or India during the monsoon season, that stream shown as a capillary line on the map will have transformed into a ranging torrent, rendering you trapped for weeks. Where possible also try to avoid severe winter weather; in addition to parts of Europe, the northern parts of Iran and the mountain passes through Turkey are often blocked by snow. To avoid being caught out by severe weather conditions, and possibly being forced to abandon your expedition, the departure date is critical: you must get it right.

With regard to visas, we secured what we could before departing. For countries without a consul in Singapore, we kept half a dozen mug shots to hand, and risked applying for visas en route The difficulty experienced in acquiring visas to enter Burma and Yugoslavia almost aborted the trip.

Finding an insurance company to commit to our risk was almost impossible, but after innumerable enquiries, Caledonian Insurance ran up a policy for a mere £20.00. Although we had a number of close shaves, including knocking down a sacred cow in India, we never put in for a claim.

NAVIGATION, MAPS & FUEL.

Like everything else, we shared the responsibility of navigating. Each morning we'd roughly calculate the route and distance we were aiming to cover for the day. Where conditions allowed, we continued well into the night. While on the move, the navigator also took responsibility for working out, as far as possible, where we were at any given point, and how many miles we'd clocked up. Additionally, the navigator constantly kept an eye on everything in the Jeep, looked out for hazards, and transferred petrol from the reserve tanks into the main.

Navigation tools included a well-proven British Army marching-type compass and protractor. Given that maps were not available for many of the areas we travelled through, we relied on a mismatch of large-scale pictorial wall maps. These did the job, but maps with a decent scale would have made navigating less demanding.

On the subject of maps, the width of streams and rivers is generally not to scale. Don't ever be taken in by those innocent blue capillary lines meandering between the hills; these lines don't account for rainstorms or the extent to which these rivers may swell.

In India, many of the road signs were in English, which was invaluable. However, and rightly so, milestones and signposts were invariably in the local language. We were only able to understand signposts written in English, therefore, navigation was generally the order of the day.

We also quickly realised when asking anyone in the Middle East or Asia, directions, it was essential to be prepared to answer a string of unconnected questions. For example, *'Are you wealthy?' 'Do you live in a big house?' 'Is it correct that English man only have one wife?' 'Have you met the Queen?'* We'd invariably field these questions with some outrageous reply, before pressing on.

In many countries, particularly Burma, acquiring fuel was a nightmare, and without the addition of the long-range fuel tanks, the journey would have been impossible. The distinct lack of roads in Burma meant that most things, including fuel, were transported by river, and the distances between the few existing fuel outlets were vast. Furthermore, automated fuel pumps hadn't yet arrived, and fuel was sold in five-gallon tins. The 400-mile drive across the desert wastelands from Quetta in Pakistan, to Iranian Zahedan, also lacked fuel outlets.

FIRST-AID & INSECTS.

We didn't have the fortune of being supplied with a complimentary first-aid box of remedies, and while not being irresponsible, chose to carry just essentials. We didn't carry sunblock or paper towels, medication for diarrhoea, constipation or malaria, and certainly no sterilising tablets for water, vitamin pills or luxury toiletries such as deodorant or shampoo. We did concede to buying a small jar of Tiger balm, from a Chinese herbalist just outside Rangoon. This lasted for the whole of the journey.

The contents of our first-aid kit included a roll of adhesive plaster, which was used to patch the Jeep's radiator hose, a tin of plasters, two bandages, a field dressing, aspirins and four bottles of whisky. In hindsight a few more items would have been useful, but there's little point in trying to cover for all eventualities and tucking away tablets for flatulence and travel sickness. These 'just-in-case' remedies take up valuable space which could be used for more important things.

Disregarding the occasional self-inflicted hangover, we were only ill once; Noel went down with dengue fever in Rangoon, and I had a bout of recurring malaria in Bangkok.

On the subject of mosquitoes and malaria, don't get paranoid; the common culex type of mosquito, which you are most likely to encounter doesn't carry malaria. The culprit is the female, and comparatively rare, anopheles mosquito. She is more prevalent at night, so avoid exposure of the body after dusk, and use a mosquito net.

The dipterous, blood-sucking sandfly is often accused of transmitting dengue fever and other disease. Again, it's the female which causes all the trouble! Unfortunately, their habitat is not restricted to the beach, and they are small enough to crawl through the mesh of a mosquito net. Spraying insect-repellent over the net helps, but this loses effectiveness once its dried. Should you not mind waking with a throat like a bear's armpit or being asphyxiated while asleep, then one of those slow-burning coils placed by the bed helps to deter both sandflies and mosquitoes.

Bed bugs, ticks and body lice carry several rickettsial diseases, including the acutely infectious typhus. These creatures are not exclusive to dosshouses: even when the bed linen looks crisp and inviting, take a look at the mattress. Wherever possible, be it the jungles of Thailand, the mountains of Baluchistan, or the Iranian desert, we preferred to camp.

Lastly, a note on sunburn: prevention is better than cure; keep out of it, or at the very least, ensure you are covered up, and always wear a hat. There's no point in having a first-aid kit packed with all the latest remedies, then treating the sun with disrespect while trying to cultivate a tropical tan. The irresponsibility of contracting self-inflicted heat-stroke, acute sunburn or both will prove an expensive liability to the rest of the team.

CAMPING & COOKING.

The bespoke, lean-to tent made in Singapore's Arab Street didn't live up to our expectations. To stave off the rain we used to rig up a lean-to shelter by securing our waterproof poncho capes to the side of the Jeep. Generally, we were often too tired to make the effort, and found sleeping under the stars an easier option.

Even in the most remote areas, safety precautions were an intuitive priority when setting up camp. For example, when setting up camp after dark, to limit the possibility of our location being detected, we'd turn off the Jeep's headlights a couple of miles before actually stopping. In this way, if we were being observed, the chances of being pinpointed were reduced.

Our morning cleaning ritual was quick and simple; teeth-cleaning and a cold 'wake-up' rinse from the tap fixed to the jerry can containing water. We never shaved while camping, and only bathed when there was a ready supply of water from a nearby river or stream.

On a journey of this nature one can't be fussy about anything – especially food. Our staple diet consisted of the tinned, ex-operational rations, supplemented with local vegetables. Often when desperately hungry and tired we'd simply open a couple of random tins and eat the food cold, straight from the can. We also regularly made 'all-ins.' This involved throwing a mix of tinned food into the pot, along with anything else that came to hand, sparked up with the essential ingredient – curry powder. We quickly became dab hands at improvising with our food supplies, and while Noel was rustling up something to eat, I'd check over the Jeep, or vice-versa.

We had three different means of cooking; a two-ring petrol cooking stove, a good supply of disposable Tommy cookers - small, round tins containing solidified methylated spirit, plus solid-fuel hexamine cooking blocks complete with their collapsible metal stands. The Tommy cookers and hexamine blocks both provided enough fuel to boil a pot of hot water or make a quick meal.

Given the relative small amount of food to eat, evening meals were always over quickly. To idle away the long and often cold nights we'd make endless mugs of tea using condensed milk, which was supplied in a tube rather like toothpaste. For drinks on the move, we used flasks which were filled each morning. Flasks are such delicate things, but surprisingly ours survived the journey. To slake our thirst in hot climates, a canvas bucket filled with water was tied onto the side of the Jeep. Throughout the course of the day, and particularly in overtly rugged terrain, some of this water was lost, but when dipping into the bucket, there was always a drink to hand.

Finance. To minimise expenses we carried only essential items, many of which were purchased from shady places such as Singapore's Arab Street, where a bargain was guaranteed. We were also actively engaged on jungle operations while planning the journey, and by inflating the number of ration packs needed for our respective platoons, built up a stock of tinned food and equipment.

The international currency of soap and cigarettes, tinned food and clothing proved invaluable and allowed us to pay our way during a time when bankers' cards didn't exist, traveller's cheques were little-known, and acquiring local currency was otherwise impossible.

The total expenditure for the trip was roughly offset, since on completion fo the journey we received cash instead of our passage home, and sold the Jeep. We were also on paid leave and therefore accrued three months' salary. All told, we just about broke even, and possibly made a profit.

Jeep	£245.00*
Third party insurance.	£20.00
Visas and related incidentals.	£40.00
Traveller's cheques – £200.00 each.	£400.00
Cash – mix of sterling and US dollars.	£80.00
TOTAL EXPENDITURE	£785.00

*Including a complete overhaul, the addition of long-range fuel tanks and spares.

APPENDIX II

THE WILLYS JEEP

HISTORY & SPECIFICATION

In November 1940, Willys-Overland of Toledo, USA, built a prototype 4x4 vehicle concurrently with Ford, and delivered it to the US Army. Due to the heavy engine, which was at the core of the vehicle's design, the 'Quad' was overweight. Its ample power output, however, made it the favoured choice over the other two vehicle manufacturers, Bantham and Ford, who were also bidding for the military contract. For initial evaluation, the US Army ordered 1,500 Willy's (Model MA). Shortly after, another fifty vehicles were ordered, some of which had four-wheel-drive.

Following some modifications, the Willys product became the standard vehicle (Model MB). Willys first contract with the US Army for this amended model totalled 16,000 vehicles. Willys produced a total of 359,850 (Model MB) vehicles up to the end of the Second World War. During this time, Bantham and Ford were producing a similar vehicle, which meant some 500,000 'General Purpose War Trucks' were manufactured during the war years.

The down side to this popular ¼ ton 4x4 vehicle was its long name. Believed to be derived from the phrase'General Purpose War Truck', the initials 'G P' naturally distorted into 'Jeep' and somewhat by accident, a brand was born. The longevity of this brand name has truly stood the test of time, so much so, that today other makes of four-wheel-drive are often referred to as 'Jeep.'

The Willys (MB) Jeep used for this journey was made in the USA then shipped to India, where it was used by the British military up until 1948. Thereafter it was shipped to Malaya, where again it was used by the British military. In 1956, having seen good service, it was sold as scrap to Soong & Company in Malaya.

History & technical specification courtesy of Mark Askew, Jeep Books Limited.

JEEP SPECIFICATION

• WILLYS JEEP	Model CJ-3B.
• Chassis No.	P 55/V/102.
• Engine No.	PV. 32758.
• Registration No.	JA 6178.
• Year of manufacture	1943.
• Engine	4-cylinder inline side valve.
• Bore and stroke	79.38 x 111.13.
• Volume	2200 cc.
• HP	54 hp at 4000 rpm.
• Length	32 inches.
• Wheel base	80 inches.
• Height	70 inches/canvas hood frame erect.
• Height	52 inches/canvas hood frame down.
• Weight	2,453 lbs.
• Maximum pay load	800 lbs.
• Gross weight (loaded)	3,253 lbs.
• Maximum fording depth	21 inches.
• Fuel consumption	18/20 mpg. Due to the extreme conditions, and excessive use of four-wheel-drive, we averaged14/15 mpg.

- Capacities [US measurements]:

Engine crankcase	5 qt
Cooling system	11 qt
Fuel tank	15 gallon [12 ½ imperial]
Jerry can	4½ gallon [1 jerry can = standard. 2 additional jerry cans added].

- Max. speed/transfer case High gear: / Max. speed/transfer case Low gear:

Max. speed/transfer case High gear:		Max. speed/transfer case Low gear:	
1st gear	24 mph	1st gear	12 mph
2nd gear	41 mph	2nd gear	21 mph
3rd gear	65 mph	3rd gear	33 mph
Reverse	18 mph	Reverse	9 mph

Although in need of significant repair, and not designed for long-haul expeditions, we could see the Jeep in Soong's scrapyard had potential. Stripped down to its last nut and bolt, Soong's mechanics made the following modifications:

The Jeep's existing jerry can was used for fuel. To optimise the fuel capacity, two long-range fuel tanks (cannibalised from an ex-army lorry), were mounted to the rear. A pipe was then rigged up to the main fuel tank under the front seat, so that by the turn of a tap, and without stopping, petrol could be transferred from either of these two tanks, into the main. In total the fuel capacity was 45 gallons.

To carry water, the spare wheel and corresponding bracket was moved from the back to the passenger side and two more jerry cans mounted to the rear alongside the original. This enabled us to carry nine gallons of water.

To keep out the rain and compensate for the lack of doors, canvas 'roller blinds' were fixed on both sides. These looked most fetching, but didn't prevent us from getting soaked. Driving mirrors were also fitted on the side of each wing.The standard Jeep tyres did the job; heavy-tread, multi-grip, quick-stop, non-slip, and all-that-jazz tyres just weren't available.

APPENDIX III

INVENTORY

Given the restricted space and weight allowance, deciding what to take, particularly when it came to spare parts, was difficult. With the exception of not carrying a spare chassis, our final selection was about right. Jeep spares were also available in some of the most unlikely places.

JEEP SPARES

Carburettor	1 complete carburettor.
Coil	1 spare coil.
Distributor	1 spare distributor.
Fan belt	2 spare fan belts.
Gaskets	1 complete set of engine gaskets and joints
Headlights	2 sealed beams.
Hose	Rubber hose for cooling system (top and lower one of each).
Inner tube	2 spare inner tubes.
Jubilee clips	Assortment.
Petrol pump	1 complete petrol pump, plus spare diaphragm.
Points	1 set of points, condenser, and set of spark plugs.
Spring	1 complete spring, two main spring leaves, four spring shackles.
Starter motor	1 starter motor.
Wheels	1 spare wheel – standard supply.

JEEP-RELATED EQUIPMENT

Axe	1 axe standard supply.
Cord	Yards of nylon parachute cord – ideal for rigging up a basha etc.
Fire extinguisher	1 fire extinguisher.
Foot pump	1 foot pump.
Glue	1 tube of glue – used for punctures.
Jerry cans	3 jerry cans.
Liquid metal	1 tube liquid metal.
Nuts and bolts	Assortment.
Oil	Always tried to keep one full can (4 pints).
Puncture kit	1 complete puncture kit.
Snorkel	1 snorkel – improvised from a piece of rubber hose and fitted to the exhaust when crossing deep rivers.
Spade	1 spade – standard supply.
Syphon tube	1 syphon tube.
Tow rope	2 good lengths of hemp tow rope.
Winch	1 hand-operated winch complete with wire rope.

CAMPING EQUIPMENT & MISCELLANEOUS ESSENTIALS.

Blankets*	2 blankets each.
Camera	1 camera plus several reels of film.
Camp beds*	2 safari camp beds.
Candles	1 box of candles.

Canvas bucket	1 – tied onto the Jeep for drinking water.
Cooking stove*	1 double-burner petrol stove.
Cooking stove*	Supply of disposable Tommy cookers and hexamine cooking blocks.
Compass*	1 ex-army good-quality marching compass.
Cooking utensils*	2 tin plates plus pots/pans/cutlery/tin opener.
Field glasses	1 pair.
First aid kit	See Appendix I. Page 190.
Flashes*	Dozen thunder flashes to warn off potential intruders – we decided against carrying firearms.
Flasks	2 vacuum flasks used almost daily.
Food*	Approximately 6 weeks supply of tinned 'operational rations.'
Goggles	2 pairs of ex-army goggles – one each – proved indispensable.
Maps	Miscellaneous range of wall maps.
Matches	Supply of matches.
Mosquito nets*	2 mosquito nets.
Parangs	2 parangs – one each.
Penknife	2 penknives.
Poncho capes*	2 rubberised poncho capes used as ground sheets/emergency shelters.
Rucksack*	2 one each packed with survival kit and ready for emergency use.
Soap	For bartering – a small amount for own use.
Tent	1 bespoke 'lean-to' tent.

Tool box	1 tool box with miscellaneous tools .
Water bottle	2 water bottles.

TOILETRIES & CLOTHING

Blazer	For the rare occasions when it was important to look presentable we both carried a blazer, pair of slacks, shoes, shirt and tie.
Duffle coats	1 each, purchased in Arab Street, Singapore. Not ideal, but the best form of outerwear we could find for cold conditions.
Footwear	1pair each of: jungle boots, heavy-duty 'ammunition boots,' flip-flops and plimsolls.
Jungle greens*	Several sets each of Malay police-issue combat clothing.
Shaving kit	1 each, containing razor blades, toothbrush, towel, comb and soap.
Socks	Infinite supply - useful for bartering.
Underpants	Endless pairs of disposable underpants, purchased, and made to order, from a used parachute in Arab Street, Singapore.

* Acquired by inflating platoon ration packs. (Courtesy of Her Majesty's Government).

APPENDIX IV

A NOTE ON DOC.

Doc, one of the seven dwarfs from Walt Disney's Snow White, was a childhood toy, manufactured by Chad Valley. In sharing my life, he's circumnavigated the world several times in the Merchant Navy, and seen active service in the Malay Emergency.

Doc was also with me during my time as Commander of Fort Brooke. Tucked away in the Malay jungle, Fort Brooke was some 2,300ft above sea level, on the Perak-Kelantan border. The area was inhabited by the Temiar Senoi aborigines, who were believed to be under Communist terrorist influence; my objective was to win them over. The bond established with Mentri Awol, the headman at Fort Brooke, was later crucial in saving my life, but it was a steep learning curve, and I didn't always get things right.

On one occasion, I agreed with Mentri, that a tribe of some 90 aborigines could take sanctuary in the fort. Mentri initially brought some of his elders to my quarters, where I plied them with fags and biscuits. Everything seemed to be running smoothly until I tuned in my wireless for a news update, and they dropped the biscuits and fled; the aborigines had assumed Doc, who was innocently perched on the wireless, was talking! Nothing would persuade them otherwise, and after a few weeks of making cautious daily visits to collect their rations, they settled near the fort, on their own ladang and fended for themselves.

APPENDIX V

BORDER CROSSINGS FROM THAILAND INTO BURMA

1: WIANG PHRAN [20° 24n 99° 52e]

625 miles north of Bangkok. This crossing continues on to the Burmese town of Kengtun via the ancient city of Chiang Mai.

2: MAE SOT [16° 38n 98° 36e]

410 miles northwest of Bangkok. This crossing traverses the Dawana mountains to Kawkareik and on to the Burmese port of Moulmein.

3: THREE PAGODAS PASS [15° 05n 98° 27e]

225 miles northwest of Bangkok. This crossing leads to the Burmese coastal town of Ye.

APPENDIX VI

ROUTE MILEAGE

The distance from the infamous Raffles Hotel in Singapore to my less renowned watering hole, The George, in Stoke-on-Trent, is approximately 13,000 miles. The route and mileage are broken down into nine different stages.

Due to the development of roads, bypasses, bridges and tunnels, which in turn has seen an explosive development of related service facilities to cope with the increase in world traffic, the distance plotted between some places on our route, may not match with that of the present day.

In Thailand, where we zigzagged our way for several days through the uncharted jungles of the Kra peninsula, there is now a highway from the Malay frontier, which carves its way through this rainforest, to Bangkok: the near-impossible journey we made in 1958, is now a leisurely weekend drive. This more direct route has clearly reduced the mileage to the Thai capital, but it must be infinitely less fun.

In Malaya, there's now an expressway from Johore Bahru, at the southern tip of the country, to Alor Star in the north. Similarly, in Istanbul, the Atatürk and Galata bridges, which span the Golden Horn and link Asia to Europe, provide a quick, alternative option to taking the ferry.

Over the last 30 years, road developments have created shortcuts and reduced the distance, but not always the driving time between places. In turn, it is now comparatively easy to access most of the countries along the route we took from Singapore to England. As the letter overleaf shows, Burma is possibly an exception: acquiring a visa to enter Burma by land route is still impossible – unless of course, you happen to know someone with the 'right' connections.

Dated. 10 June 2002

Dear Mr. S. R. Follows,

With the reference of our telephone conversation and your letter dated 31 May 2002 enquiring about your trip from Singapore to England, and I would like to reply to you that our visas not allow the visitors travelling through the land route crossing the border areas.

I am pleased to enclose some Myanmar Tourist Information leaflets which will be useful for your next tourist trips to our country.

Yours sincerely,

Kyaw Nyunt Lwin
Second Secretary
Consular Section,
Embassy of the Union of Myanmar.

Letter from the Burmese Embassy, London.

STAGE 1

Singapore to the Malay-Thai frontier.

	STAGE MILES	CUMULATIVE MILES
Singapore - Johore Bahru, Malaya	17	17
Johore Bahru - Kuala Lumpur	252	269
Kuala Lumpur - Alor Star	321	590
Alor Star - Sadau	43	633
TOTAL STAGE MILES		**633**

STAGE 2

Malay-Thai frontier to the Burmese frontier.

	STAGE MILES	CUMULATIVE MILES
Sadau - Songkhla	61	61
Songkhla - Renong	425	486
Renong - Chumporn	96	582
Chumporn - Bangkok	315	897
Bangkok - Chainat	216	1113
Chainat -Tak	196	1309
Tak-Burmese frontier	77	1386
TOTAL STAGE MILES		**1386**

STAGE 3

Burmese-Thai frontier to India.

	STAGE MILES	CUMULATIVE MILES
Mae Sot - Moulmein	184	184
Moulmein - Thaton	71	255
Thaton -Sittang	67	322
Sittang -Rangoon	99	421
Rangoon - Mandalay	444	865
Mandalay - Maymo	49	914
Maymo - Lashio	139	1053
Lashio - Mong Yu	125	1178
Mong Yu - Myitkyina	221	1399
Myitkyina - [Start of] The Ledo Road	70	1469
[Start of] The Ledo Road - Indian Frontier	237	1706
TOTAL STAGE MILES		**1706**

STAGE 4

Indian frontier to the Pakistan frontier.

	STAGE MILES	CUMULATIVE MILES
Indian frontier - Dibrugarh	115	115
Dibrugarh - Goalpara	395	510
Goalpara - Jopihaghat	[Ferry across the Brahmaputra]	
Jopihaghat -Darjeeling	265	775
Darjeeling - Siliguri	107	882
Siliguri - Dalkhola	129	1011
Dalkhola - Khajuria Ghat	156	1167
K.Ghat - ?	[Ferry across the Ganges to unknown place]*	
Unknown place - Arsonal	140	1307
Arsonal - Allahabad	391	1698
Allahabad - Kawnpore	189	1887
Kawnpore - Delhi	303	2190
Delhi - Pakistan frontier	315	2505
TOTAL STAGE MILES		**2505**

*Arrived miles off course at unknown place on the Ganges.

STAGE 5

Indian-Pakistan frontier to Iran.

	STAGE MILES	CUMULATIVE MILES
Indian-Pakistan frontier - Lahore	29	29
Lahore - Multan	215	244
Multan -Dera Ghazi Khan [DGK]	106	350
DGK - Quetta	269	619
Quetta -Dalbandin	223	842
Dalbandin -Iranian frontier	211	1053
TOTAL STAGE MILES		**1053**

STAGE 6

Iran to Turkey.

	STAGE MILES	CUMULATIVE MILES
Iranian frontier -Bam	283	283
Bam -Kerman	128	411
Kerman - Yazd	317	728
Yazd - Isfahan	273	1001
Isfahan -Tehran	265	1266
Tehran - Qazvin	94	1360
Qazvin - Tabriz	443	1803
Tabriz - Turkish frontier	212	2015
TOTAL STAGE MILES		**2015**

STAGE 7
Turkey to Greek frontier.

	STAGE MILES	CUMULATIVE MILES
Turkish frontier- Erzurum	198	198
Erzurum - Trabzon	193	391
Trabzon - Samsun	219	610
Samsun - Ankara	205	815
Ankara -Istanbul	304	1119
Istanbul - Greek frontier	161	1280
TOTAL STAGE MILES		**1280**

STAGE 8
Greece to Yugoslavia.

	STAGE MILES	CUMULATIVE MILES
Greek frontier - Alexandropolis	97	97
Alexandropolis - Thessalonika	215	312
Thessalonika - Yugoslav frontier	71	383
Yugoslav frontier - Nis	281	664
Nis - Belgrade	180	884
TOTAL STAGE MILES		**844**

STAGE 9

Yugoslavia - England

	STAGE MILES	CUMULATIVE MILES
Belgrade - Zagreb	263	263
Zagreb - Salzburg	260	523
Salzburg - Munich	117	640
Munich - Paris	539	1179
Paris - London	265	1444
London - Stoke-on-Trent	151	1595
TOTAL STAGE MILES		**1595**

TOTAL CUMULATIVE MILES

STAGE 1 Singapore - Malay-Thai frontier	633
STAGE 2 Malay-Thai frontier - Burmese frontier	1386
STAGE 3 Burmese-Thai frontier - India	1706
STAGE 4 Indian frontier -Pakistan frontier	2505
STAGE 5 Indian-Pakistan frontier - Iran	1053
STAGE 6 Iran -Turkey	2015
STAGE 7 Turkey - Greek frontier	1280
STAGE 8 Greek frontier - Yugoslavia	844
STAGE 9 Yugoslavia - England	1595
TOTAL CUMULATIVE MILES	**13017**

AFGHANISTAN
IRAN
Kerman
Bam
Zahedan
Quetta
Multan
Lahore
THE INDUS
THE GANGES
PAKISTAN
Delhi
NEPAL
Allahabad
Gulf of Oman
OMAN
INDIA
YEMEN
Arabian Sea
Gulf of Aden
THE MALDIVES
Route
Frontiers/Border crossings
Ferry boarding/disembarking
Main Rivers
Main cities, towns and villages en route
The Raffles Hotel